Graded in Qur'an Reading

The 'Uthmani Script

Graded Steps in Qur'an Reading

The 'Uthmani Script

Teacher's/Self-Study Edition

Compiled by
AbdulWahid Hamid

MELS

بِسْمِ ٱللَّهِ ٱلرَّحْمَٰنِ ٱلرَّحِيمِ

إِنَّآ
أَنزَلْنَٰهُ
قُرْءَٰنًا عَرَبِيًّا
لَّعَلَّكُمْ تَعْقِلُونَ

In the name of Allah,
the Most Gracious, the Ever Merciful

We have indeed sent it down
as an Arabic Qur'ān
that you may use your minds.

The Qur'ān - Sūrah Yūsuf, 12: 2

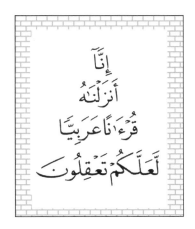

Published by MELS
Muslim Education & Literary Services,

www.melspublications.com
Email: **orders@melspublications.com**
Freephone: 0800 081 1942

www.melsamerica.com
Email in USA: **MelsAmerica@gmail.com**

First Published 2001
This Reprint 2015

ISBN 0 948196 18 1 (Teacher's/Self-Study Edition)

Arabic typesetting and computer support
Abdulkader Khattab
Cover design Imtiaze A Manjra
Graphic design consultant Zafar A Malik

Printed and bound by
Gutenberg Press, Malta

Contents

..Continued

Contents

Transliteration of Arabic into English

Long vowels

Long vowels are written as:
ā or *aa* as in lām or laam
ī or *ee* or *ii* as in mīm. meem or miim
ū or *oo* or *uu* as in nūn, noon or nuun.

Heavy consonants

A dot is placed under certain letters to denote Arabic letters that are pronounced with a thick or heavy sound:
ص Ṣ or ṣ for ṣaad as in Ṣalaah
ض Ḍ or ḍ for ḍaad as in Wuḍū'
ط Ṭ or ṭ for ṭā' as in Ṭāhā
ظ Ẓ or ẓ for ẓā' as in Ẓuhr.

Other letters

ح Ḥ or ḥ as in the word Fat-ḥah (pronounced with a strong expulsion of breath.

ع An open inverted comma (') represents 'Ayn as in 'aṣri.

ء A closed inverted comma (') denotes Hamzah as in Mu'min.

For further explanation and for English equivalents of other Arabic letters, see Unit 6, page 24.

Introduction

This is a concise, step-by step manual for learning to read the Qur'ānic script. It is intended for self-study and for use by teachers.

The script used in this book is based on the Uthmānī script. (The earlier edition, *Easy Steps in Qur'ān Reading*, uses the Majīdī script which is common in the sub-continent and which in many respects is helpful for a beginner.)

There are four main reasons for using the 'Uthmānī script:
1. The system of signs and vowelling in this script conforms to the way the Qur'ān was recited by the Tabi'ī scholar, 'Aṣim ibn Abi-n Najūd. His recitation can be traced back to the noble Prophet, peace be on him, through an authentic and uninterrupted chain of narrators including 'Uthmān ibn 'Affān, 'Alī ibn Abī Ṭālib, Zayd ibn Thābit and Ubayy ibn Ka'b among the Companions of the Prophet.

2. The script with its system of signs and vowelling makes understanding and following the rules of *tajwīd* very precise. Tajwīd is the art and the science of reciting the Qur'ān. Initially, in some instances, this script may appear to be more difficult but the end result is greater clarity and precision.

3. The 'Uthmānī script is becoming more familiar throughout the world with the wide distribution of copies of the Qur'ān printed in the Middle East such as the Madīnah Muṣ-ḥaf which is elegantly and beautifully written by the Damascene calligrapher 'Uthmān Ṭāhā.

4. Familiarity with and mastering of the script used in this Muṣ-ḥaf will help in the further study of Arabic as a language.

The layout of this manual is similar to that of the first edition which has proved to be helpful to both teachers and students. There are 48 Units, each having up to 9 lines of Arabic text on the right hand page with explanatory notes in English on the facing page. A full audio recording of the Arabic text is available. The recording identifies the number of the Unit and each line of text to enable the user to follow the recording and text quite easily.

With the text and the recording, it should be possible to learn to read the Arabic script through self-study. However, the help of a competent teacher will certainly make learning much easier and quicker. Such help is indeed necessary with some of the finer points of pronunciation.

Introduction

This manual can be used together with the other materials in the MELS *Easy Steps in Arabic* course. These include the Alphabet Summary Chart, Flashcards and the two workbooks, *Easy Steps in Arabic Handwriting*. These workbooks are carefully graded and only words from the Qur'ān are used.

It is worth stressing the importance of learning to write the Arabic script as well. This is a necessary skill in its own right as a basis for the further study of Arabic as a language. Writing also helps tremendously in the process of mastering the reading of the script. Reading and writing should proceed together. The first Section of this manual fits neatly with the simultaneous use of Workbook One of *Easy Steps in Arabic Handwriting*, and gives users a feeling of rapid achievement.

We strongly recommend that learning to read and write the Arabic script and learning the basics of reading the Qur'ān should be done in an intensive manner over three to four weeks. An Appendix on 'How to use this book' gives some suggestions for self-study and hints on teaching techniques. After this, of course, a great deal of further practice, listening to good recitations and paying attention to detail, are all necessary in order to recite the Qur'ān accurately and beautifully.

Persons who are able to read and write the script can then go on to understand the language of the Qur'ān. For this, the MELS *Access to Qur'ānic Arabic* course should provide a good foundation.

In preparing this manual, I have relied heavily on *Tajwīd-ul-Qur'ān* by Ashraf Abdul-Fattah, Aladdin Hassanin and Salah Saleh, London, 1989. It is an outstanding work of meticulous scholarship which shows the authors' grasp of the elements of both Arabic and English phonetics. Also, the notes in Arabic at the end of the Madīnah Muṣ-ḥaf are both precise and succinct.

We hope and pray, *in shā' Allāh,* that this effort will contribute to the more widespread and regular reading of the Glorious Qur'ān and that through it, many will continue on the great and important task of learning Arabic as a language in order to understand God's only authentic Reminder to us and to feel something of the joy and serenity of having it as a constant companion.

'AbdulWāḥid Ḥāmid
Muḥarram 1422, March 2001

SECTION ONE

Quick Start

Notes for Unit 1

Arabic is written and read from the right to the left. There are 28 letters in the alphabet.

The first letter (line 2 opposite) is Alif: ا . As a consonant, Alif is written with a hamzah (ء) above or below it: أ and إ .

In line 3 opposite, Alif with the hamzah is written with short vowels. The hamzah on its own is also written with vowels. (For pronunciation, listen to the recording.)

The second letter is ب - Baa'. It is equivalent to a B in English. In its complete form, it has a flat base and one dot below. In line 5 opposite, the letter ب is written with short vowels.

Short vowels

There are three short vowels in Arabic: **a**, **i** and **u**.

The vowel **'a'** (***fat-ḥah*** in Arabic) is a small slanting stroke above a letter. With all the letters opposite, the vowel **'a'** is sounded as the *a* in *cat:*

بَ = Ba

The vowel **'i'** (***kasrah*** in Arabic) is a small slanting stroke below a letter. It is sounded as the *i* in *pin*:

بِ = Bi

The vowel **'u'** (***ḍammah*** in Arabic) is a hook, like a large comma, above a letter. It is sounded as the *u* in *pull*:

بُ = Bu

In line 6, is the letter ج - Jeem. It is equal to a J in English and pronounced as the *j* in *jam.*

In line 8, is the letter د - Daal. It is equal to a D in English and pronounced as the *d* in *delta.*

The Alif and the Hamzah

In line 3 is the Alif with a hamzah and the vowels ***a***, ***i*** and ***u***.

The ء is also written on its own with a vowel ***a***, ***i*** or ***u***.

أ or إ is sounded as a short 'catch' from the back of the throat - followed by the vowel sound.

أَ is pronounced like the *a* in *at*. So is ءَ .

إِ is pronounced like the *i* in *inner*. So is ءِ .

أُ is pronounced like the *u* in *ummah*. So is ءُ.

A B J D

أ ب ج and د

are the first four letters in the old arrangement of the Arabic alphabet known as ***abjadiyyah***. This arrangement is still used for numbering, as in the pages of Notes at the back of the Madīnah Muṣ-ḥaf.

بِسۡمِ ٱللَّهِ ٱلرَّحۡمَٰنِ ٱلرَّحِيمِ 1

ا ء 2

أَ إِ أُ ءَ ءِ ءُ 3

ب 4

بَ بِ بُ 5

ج 6

جَ جِ جُ 7

د 8

دَ دِ دُ 9

Notes for Unit 2

New letters

Three new letters are introduced in line 1 opposite.

The letter Waaw (و) is equivalent to the English 'W'.

The letter Yaa' (ى) is equivalent to the English 'Y'. It is the last letter in the alphabet.

The letter Taa' (ت) is sounded as the *t* in *tan*. It has the same shape as a Baa' but has two dots on top. The number and position of dot(s) is vital in distinguishing one letter from another.

Joining letters

The letters are shown in line 1 written separately and as they are when joined to another letter. Note that:

1. Some letters, like ا , و and د, do not change their basic shape. These three letters are never joined to a following letter - see Unit 3 also.

2. Other letters, like ب , ت and ج have a main body and a tail. The tail is cut off when these letters are joined to a following letter: بـ , تـ and جـ .

3. The letter ى in its shortened form is changed completely to يـ It then has the same shape as a shortened Baa' but with two dots below. In its separate form, in the Madīnah Muṣ-ḥaf, ى is always written without dots.

Long vowels

1. A bare Alif is one without a hamzah or a vowel.
A bare Alif lengthens the vowel *a*.
بَ = Ba; بَا = Baa
The vowel thus lengthened is twice the length of the short vowel in pronunciation.
بَا may be transliterated as Baa or Bā. In transliteration into English, a stroke or bar above a vowel, shows a long vowel.

2. A bare ى lengthens the vowel *i* :
بِ = Bi;

بِى = Biy, sounded as *'bee'* in *beef.*

بِى may be transliterated as Bee, Bii or Bī. It is written as بِيـ when joined to a following letter.

3. A bare و lengthens the vowel *u*:
بُ = Bu; بُو = Buw, sounded as *'boo'* in *'boot'*.

بُو may be transliterated as Boo or Bū.

Written but not pronounced

In line 9, the final Alif in the words جَابُواْ and أُوتُواْ has a small circle above it.

An اْ وْ or ىْ with a small circle is not pronounced.

ا و ى ب ت ج د 1
ـا ـو يـ بـ تـ جـ ـد

بَ بَا تَ تَا جَ جَا دَ دَا 2

بِ بِى تِ تِى جِ جِى دِ دِى 3

بُ بُو تُ تُو جُ جُو دُ دُو 4

أَبَ أَبَا أَبِ أَبِى أَبُ أَبُو 5

أَبَتِ وَجَبَ وَجَدَ وُجِدَ يَجِدُ تَجِدُ 6

بَابَ تَابَ بَاتَ جَاءَ تَبَابَ ءَابَاءِ 7

جِيدِ بَادِى تَبِيدَ أُجِيبُ يُجِيبُ 8

جُودِى وَدُودُ جَابُواْ أُوتُواْ 9

Notes for Unit 3

'Selfish' Letters

In writing Arabic, the six letters

ا د ذ ر ز and و

are never joined to a following letter. Call them the 'Selfish Letters' if you like.

In line 6, the letter ح - Ḥaa' is pronounced with a strong and sustained expulsion of breath.

The vowel 'a' on a حَ is sounded as the a in art.

Tanwin

Tanwīn means adding an 'n' sound to a vowel 'a', 'i' and 'u'.
Tanwīn only occurs at the end of words.

(i) The extra stroke above the vowel 'a' represents the 'n', for example:

دَ = Da   دً = Dan

Note the difference between this and the sound of the English word 'Dan'.

After tanwīn with the vowel 'a' (called *fat-ḥah tanwīn*), an alif is written but not pronounced when the 'an' is pronounced, as in:

أَبَدًا = a Ba Dan

In some cases, no alif is written after fat-ḥah tanwīn - see Unit 14.
The fat-ḥah tanwīn is written in two ways in the Madīnah Muṣ-ḥaf:
(a) directly above the fat-ḥah as above ـً;
(b) staggered as ـً . For the significance of this, see Unit 14.

(ii) An extra stroke under a final vowel 'i' (called *kasrah tanwīn*) produces an 'n' sound, for example:

دِ = Di   يَدٍ = Ya Din

The tanwīn with the vowel 'i' is written either directly below the kasrah as above, or staggered as ـٍ. For more details, see Unit 15.

(iii) An extra inverted hook after a final vowel 'u' (called *ḍammah tanwīn*) produces an 'n' sound,
for example:

دُ = Du   يَدٌ = Ya Dun

The tanwīn is also written side by side with the vowel 'u' as ـٌ. For the significance of this, see Unit 16.

ا د ذ ر ز و 1

أَ إِ أُ دَ دِ دُ ذَ ذِ ذُ 2

رَ رِ رُ زَ زِ زُ وَ وِ وُ 3

أَرَ تَرَ يَرَ ذُو ذَا ذِى ذَاتَ ذَوَاتَ 4

زَارَ يَزُورُ بَاتَ يَبِيتُ تَابَ يَتُوبُ 5

ح حَ حِ حُ حَـ حِـ حُـ 6

يَدٌ تَاجٌ رِيحٌ حِجَابٌ أُجَاجٌ 7

أَبَدًا وَاحِدًا زُورًا زَبُورًا ثُبُورًا 8

يَدٍ جَازٍ حَرَجٍ خَبَرٍ ثُبَاتٍ 9

Notes for Unit 4

New letters

In line 1 opposite is the letter ث - Thaa'. It is the fourth letter of the alphabet. It has the same shape as the Baa' and Taa' but has three dots above. It is pronounced as the *th* in *thank*.

The letter خ - KHaa' (line 2) has the same shape as the ج and ح. KHaa' has one dot above. It is sounded as a grating sound from the palate or roof of the mouth.
The vowel 'a' on a KHaa' خَ is sounded like the *o* in *cot*, producing a rounded 'khau' sound.

The Sukun

A sukūn is a symbol (ـْ) above a letter resembling the head of a small Ḥaa'. (In modern Arabic, it is written as a small circle.)

A letter with a sukūn has no vowel of its own and is therefore called **a vowelless letter.**

The function of a sukūn is to join in pronunciation the letter over which it occurs to the previous letter and vowel to form **one syllable**.

تُ = Tu تُبْ = TuB

أَحْبَبْتَ = aḤ BaB Ta

The Shaddah

A shaddah is a small (ـّ) sign placed above a letter. (It is of course written from right to left.)

The Shaddah joins and doubles:

1. It joins in pronunciation the letter above which it occurs to the preceding letter and vowel.
2. The letter above which it occurs is then repeated and pronounced with its own vowel.

رَبَّ = RaB Ba and is pronounced with a heavy stress on the B. The two syllables - RaB and Ba - must be distinct.
The effect of the Shaddah is to place a strong emphasis on the letter it doubles.

In line 9, the letters ل - Laam and هـ - Haa' occur in the word لهب.
ل is equivalent to the English L.

One difference between a ل and an ا is that Laam is joined to a following letter whereas Alif is not.

هـ is an H pronounced from the back of the throat, but (unlike ح) with no breeze.

The wavy sign ـٓ in line 9 is called a maddah. It further lengthens the vowel sound.

1 ث ثَ ثِ ثُ ثـَ ثـِ ثـُ

2 خ خَ خِ خُ خـَ خـِ خـُ

3 أَثَرِ خَبُثَ خَرَجَ خَرَاجُ خَبِيثَ أَخُ أَثَاثًا

4 تُبْ زِدْ ذَرْ إِذْ أَوْ تُـجِبْ رَبِحَتْ جَاوَزْ

5 بَدْرِ تَحْتَ أُخْتِ يَشْرِبُ أَحْبَبْتَ بَرْزَخٌ

6 بَيْتِ حَيْثُ خَيْرٌ رَيْبَ زَوْجًا رَوْحٌ

7 رَبَّ حَجَّ تَبَّ تَبَّتَ أَيِّ حُبًّا بَثَّ

8 يُحِبُّ تُحِبُّ ثَبِّتَ جَبَّارٍ تُحَدِّثُ يُدَبِّرُ

9 تَبَّتْ يَدَآ أَبِى لَهَبٍ وَ تَبَّ

Notes for Unit 5

More new letters

س - Seen, is sounded as the *s* in *seen*.

ش - Sheen, is as the *sh* in *sheen*.

ف - Faa', is as the *f* in *fax*.

ل - Laam, is as the *l* in *lamb*.

م - Meem, is as the *m* in *mean*.

ن - Noon, is as the *n* in *noon*.

هـ - Haa', is close to the *h* in *hat*. *It is, however, different from the English* *'h'* in that it is sounded from the back of the throat.

Lines 1 and 2 show the above letters in their separate and shortened forms.

The tail of the س , ش , ف , ل and م is cut when each of these letters is joined to a following letter.

ث and ش

Sheen in its shortened form - شـ - must be distinguished from ثـ , Thaa'.

> The letter Haa' is written in four different ways:
>
> ه separately;
>
> هـ joined to a following letter;
>
> ـهـ when joined to a preceding and following letter;
>
> ـه at the end of a word.

ب and ن

In its shortened form, the ن is reduced to the basic shape of a shortened Baa'. The ن however has its dot above.

ذ and ن

One difference between a shortened Noon and a DHaal is that the Noon is joined to a following letter whereas DHaal is not. Identify the letters in the following:

مذبذبين منيبين نبات ذنوبنا

Note that the ف has a big head, a flat base, and one dot above.

In line 3, the Alif with a small circle in تَجَسَّسُواْ is not pronounced.

In line 7, notice the small oval shape on the final alif in أَنَاْ This alif is thus ignored in pronunciation and does not lengthen the preceding vowel 'a'.

In line 9, there is a hamzah with a sukūn over the wāw in مُؤْمِنِينَ .
This indicates that the first syllable - مُؤْ - is to be cut short abruptly and not lengthened at all.
For more examples of this, see Unit 20.

Notice the wavy sign called a **maddah;** this further lengthens the final vowel in إِنَّآ - pronounced *in-naaaa*.

1 س ش ف ل م ن ه

2 سـ شـ فـ لـ مـ نـ... هـ...ـهـ...ـه

3 سَبَبٍ تَجَسَّسُواْ يُونُسُ سَبَّحَ سَلَامٌ

4 شَمْسٌ يَسْتَبْشِرُونَ فَحَشَرَ فَنَادَى

5 بَلْ هَلْ نَبَاتَ بُنيَانٌ لَيْلًا

6 هُوَ لَهْوَ لَهُ يُوَجِّهُهُ لَيْلًا وَنَهَارًا

7 هُوَ هِىَ أَنتَ أَنتِ أَنَاْ هُمْ أَنتُمْ نَحْنُ

8 وَمِن شَرِّ حَاسِدٍ إِذَا حَسَدَ

9 إِنَّآ أَرْسَلْنَا نُوحًا وَمَا هُم بِمُؤْمِنِينَ

SECTION TWO

Alphabet & Short Vowels

Notes for Unit 6

The alphabet in sequence

The sequence of the letters in the Arabic alphabet opposite is the one used in dictionaries. Memorize the letters in sequence. Note the number and position of dot(s). Listen and repeat. Pay special attention to the pronunciation of the following:

ث **th**, as in *think*

ح **ḥ**, pronounced with a strong and sustained expulsion of breath

ذ **dh**, as the *th* in *that*

ر **r**, slightly rolled as in Scottish and somewhat rounded as in *rock*

ص **ṣ**, a rounded 'ṣ' pronounced with the tip of the tongue pressing against the lower teeth and then raising the tongue to press against the palate.

ض **ḍ**, a rounded and emphatic 'ḍ' pronounced with the tip and back of the tongue against the gums of the upper front teeth and raising the tongue to press against the palate. The sound resembles the *d* in *dot*. Because of the unique heaviness of this sound, Arabic is called the 'language of the Ḍaad'.

ط **ṭ**, tongue in the same position as with 'Ḍaad'; sounded as the *ṭ* in *toss*.

ظ **ẓ**, emphatic 'ẓ' pronounced with the tip of the tongue close to the inner side of the upper teeth, with lips rounded throughout.

ع normally transliterated by an open inverted comma ('), the **'ayn** is a guttural stop produced with the constriction of the larynx. On its own, it resembles a sort of growl, but sounded properly with other letters, it is one of the sounds that makes Arabic distinctively rich and pleasant to hear.

غ **gh**, similar to the sound made in gargling with the lips slightly rounded.

ق **q**, a rounded, explosive 'k' sound produced by contact with the back of the tongue and the back of the palate.

هـ **h**, is pronounced from the back of the throat and sounds like the *h* in *hat*. It must always be breathed, even if it comes at the end of an utterance as in the word Allāh.

The Alif as a consonant is written with a hamzah above and below: أ إ
As a long vowel, the Alif is written bare, without the hamzah.
The Alif is also written with a small ṣaad above, called a hamzatu-l waṣl. For more on this, see Unit 33.

بِسۡمِ ٱللَّهِ ٱلرَّحۡمَٰنِ ٱلرَّحِيمِ 1

ا 2

ب ت ث 3

ج ح خ 4

د ذ 5

ر ز س ش ص ض 6

ط ظ ع غ ف ق 7

ك 8

ل م ن هـ و ى 9

Notes for Unit 7

Letter recognition practice

Listen to the recording of the text opposite and repeat.

Practice reading on your own after listening to the recording.

If you can read each line in ten seconds or under, you are doing fine.

For further practice, try reading each line from left to right also.

Note that the hamzah (ء) is included on its own in lines 1 and 4.

In its complete form, the Yaa' in the Madīnah Muṣ-ḥaf is written without dots as in lines 3 and 6: ى

In modern Arabic, it is written with two dots below: ي .

Old arrangement of the Arabic alphabet

In Unit 1, we mentioned the first four letters of the old arrangement of the Arabic alphabet. The complete alphabet according to this arrangement is (read from right to left):

أ ب ج د هـ و ز ح ط ى
ك ل م ن س ع ف ص
ق ر ش ت ث خ ذ ض ظ غ

This arrangement is learnt in the following words and is still used for numbering (read from right to left):

أَبَجَدْ هَوَّزْ حُطِّى كَلَمَنْ
سَعَفَصْ قَرَشَتْ ثَخَّذْ ضَظَّغْ

ا د ر ء ط ح و س هـ 1

ع ص ك ن ب ظ ج ف ذ 2

غ ط ض ز خ ق ش ى ث 3

ت ز ك ء ب س ث ص ج 4

ظ د خ ض ل ذ ط ش ف 5

هـ غ ى م ح ق ر ع و 6

ث غ م ر ج ل ق ض ح 7

أَبَجَدْ هَوِّزْ حُطِّى كَلِمَنْ 8

سَعَفَصْ قَرَشَتْ ثَخَذْ ضَظَّغْ 9

Notes for Unit 8

Letters in various forms

This Unit shows letters in their full and shortened forms. Use Units 8 and 9 as reference if you have any difficulty recognising a letter later on.

The number and position of dots are crucial in recognising some letters.

Joining letters

For the purpose of linking with other letters, Arabic letters may be divided into three types:

1. Letters that stay virtually the same, whatever their position:

ا ء د ذ ر ز ط ظ و

2. Letters which have a main body and a tail. When joined to a following letter, these letters have their tails cut off:

ب ت ث ج ح خ

س ش ص ض ع غ

ف ق ل م ن

See lines 1 - 4 opposite for these letters in their complete form and with their tails cut off.

3. Letters which change their form completely in some cases:

‘Ayn	ـع	ـعـ	عـ	ع
Ghayn	ـغ	ـغـ	غـ	غ
Kaaf	ـك	ـكـ	كـ	ك
Haa’	ـه	ـهـ	هـ	ه
Yaa’	ـى	ـيـ	يـ	ى

The six letters ا د ذ ر ز و are never joined to a following letter. We have called them ‘the Selfish Letters’.

The hamzah is written on its own, or with an alif, waaw, separate yaa’, or a yaa’ without dots.

ء أ ـأ ـئـ إ ـإ ؤ ئ

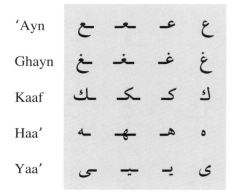

1 ب ت ث ج ح خ
بـ تـ ثـ جـ حـ خـ

2 ذ ر س ش ص ض
ـذ ـر سـ شـ صـ ضـ

3 ع غ ف ق ك ل
عـ غـ فـ قـ كـ لـ

4 م ن ه ء ى
مـ نـ هـ ئـ يـ

5 غـ لـ ئـ بـ صـ خـ فـ ثـ حـ

6 نـ ـد قـ جـ عـ تـ ضـ يـ بـ

7 جـ يـ لـ عـ ثـ ر صـ كـ غـ

8 شـ ـذ ئـ فـ ز هـ حـ قـ ضـ

9 إِيَّاكَ نَعْبُدُ وَإِيَّاكَ نَسْتَعِينُ

Notes for Unit 9

Letter recognition practice

The letter haa' with two dots above

(ـة ة) is called a taa' marbūṭah or 'tied t'.
It comes only at the ends of words, as in: بَقَرَةٌ رَقَبَةٌ

It is pronounced either as an 'h' or a 't'.
It is pronounced as an 'h' when the vowel that goes with it is not sounded.
It is pronounced as a 't' with its vowel.

The letter laam followed by an alif is written as لا or ـلا .

A small yaa' (ے) is often written after a word with a final kasrah (line 7).
It serves to lengthen the kasrah, as in:

بِهِۦ pronounced *bi hee*

Occasionally, it is written between two letters, also after a kasrah, which it lengthens, as in:

إِبْرَٰهِۦمَ pronounced *Ib raa heem.*

Lines 4 and 5 opposite show letters in their various forms.

بس تر تم جل حج خط سد شر 1

عذ صب ضد غم فذ قل كن لم 2

نك هل ئذ ير ثج نت ثب نظ 3

4	ا ـا	ب بب	ت تت	ث ثث	ع ععع	غ غغغ	ف ففف
5	ق قق	ك كك	ل + ا لالا	م ممم	ه هـهـه	ه + ت ة ـة	ى ييى

نـبـذ ثـ ة ـعـ ـة ـفـ ـغـ ـقـ نهـ 6

يـ تـ لا بلا كل مة بهۦ صة عة ئع 7

نع بق نجـ يمـن كا تى ثى بى لى 8

ٱهۡدِنَا ٱلصِّرَٰطَ ٱلۡمُسۡتَقِيمَ 9

Notes for Unit 10

The vowel 'a' - the fat-hah

The vowel 'a' - the fat-ḥah - is a slanting stroke above a letter. It is sounded in three different ways, according to the letter carrying it.

1. With the two letters حَ - Ḥaa' and عَ - Ayn,

the vowel 'a' is sounded like the *a* in *hart*.

2. With the eight letters (read from right to left)

خَ رَ صَ ضَ طَ ظَ غَ قَ

the vowel 'a' is a rounded sound like the *o* in *cot*, or the *au* in *aught*.

The vowelled لَ in the word اللّٰه - Allāh, is also sometimes pronounced rounded as 'lau'.

3. With all other letters, the fat-ḥah is sounded as the *a* in *cat*, as we have seen in Section One.

Initially, you may read the Arabic through English transliteration, for example:

جَ = Ja   سَ = Sa

أَمَرَ = a Ma Ra   صَدَقَ = Ṣa Da Qa

The stress in the words above is on the first syllable.

Or, you may adopt the direct Phonetic Method, making the beginning sound of the letter and adding the vowel sound that goes with it.

Distinguish between the sounds of the letters with the vowel 'a' in each of the groups below.

أَ عَ
تَ طَ
ثَ سَ صَ
حَ هَـ

خَ غَ
دَ ضَ
زَ ذَ ظَ
كَ قَ

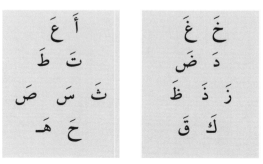

أَ بَ تَ ثَ جَ حَ خَ 1

دَ ذَ رَ زَ سَ شَ 2

صَ ضَ طَ ظَ عَ غَ فَ قَ 3

كَ لَ مَ نَ هَـ وَ ىَ 4

أَمَـرَ بَـلَـغَ ثَـمَـرَ جَـمَـعَ 5

حَسَـدَ ذَكَـرَ رَفَـعَ زَعَـمَ 6

شَـرَحَ صَـدَقَ ضَـرَبَ ظَـلَـمَ 7

عَـدَلَ قَـمَـرَ كَـسَـبَ وَجَـدَ 8

قَـنَـتَ قَـطَـرَ خَـرَجَ ذَهَـبَ 9

Notes for Unit 11

The vowel 'i' - the kasrah

The vowel 'i' - the kasrah - is a slanting stroke below a letter.
It is sounded as the *i* in *pin*.

Remember all vowel sounds on the opposite page are short.

With the alif having the hamzah below (إِ), and with the ءِ on its own the vowel 'i' is pronounced preceded by a slight 'catch' from the back of the throat. Thus, note the pronunciation of:

إِبِلِ i Bi Li   نِسَآءِ Ni Saaaa 'i   سُئِلَ Su 'i La

As with the previous page, you may initially read the Arabic through transliteration, for example:

جِ = Ji   سِ = Si

أَذِنَ = a DHi Na   بَقِيَ = Ba Qi Ya

The stress in the words above is on the first syllable.

Distinguish between the sounds of the letters with the vowel 'i' in each of the groups below.

إِ عِ	خِ غِ
تِ طِ	دِ ضِ
ثِ سِ صِ	زِ ذِ ظِ
حِ هِـ	كِ قِ

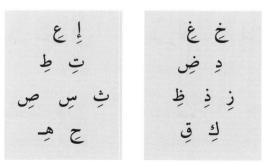

إِ بِ تِ ثِ جِ حِ خِ 1

دِ ذِ رِ زِ سِ شِ 2

صِ ضِ طِ ظِ عِ غِ فِ قِ 3

كِ لِ مِ نِ هِـ وِ يِ 4

أَذِنَ بَقِىَ حَمِدَ خَشِىَ 5

عَلِمَ شَرِبَ عَجِبَ غَضِبَ 6

كَذِبَ بَخِلَ فَلِمَ يَئِسَ 7

أَبَتِ بَلَدِ مَلِكِ حَطَبِ 8

إِبِلِ كِبَرِ سَخِرَ إِرَمَ 9

Notes for Unit 12

The vowel 'u' - the dammah

The vowel 'u' - the ḍammah - is a hook, like a large comma, placed above a letter.
It is sounded as the *u* in *pull*.

Remember all vowel sounds on the opposite page are short.

With the alif having the hamzah above (أُ), and with the ءُ on its own, the vowel 'u' is pronounced preceded by a slight 'catch' from the back of the throat.
Thus, note the pronunciation of: أُذِنَ u DHi Na

As with the previous page, the Arabic may be spelt and read thus:

جُ	= Ju	سُ	= Su
جُعِلَ	= Ju 'i La	خُلِقَ	= KHu Li Qa

The stress in the words above is on the first syllable.

Distinguish between the sounds of the letters with the vowel 'u' in each of the groups below.

أُ عُ
تُ طُ
ثُ سُ صُ
حُ هُـ

خُ غُ
دُ ضُ
زُ ذُ ظُ
كُ قُ

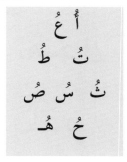

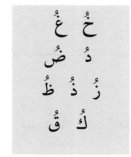

أُ بُ تُ ثُ جُ حُ خُ 1

دُ ذُ رُ زُ سُ شُ 2

صُ ضُ طُ ظُ عُ غُ فُ قُ 3

كُ لُ مُ نُ هُـ وُ ىُ 4

جُعِلَ خُلِقَ ذُكِرَ سُئِلَ 5

ظُلِمَ مُنِعَ ضُرِبَ سُقِطَ 6

وُجِدَ هُدِىَ عُفِىَ حُشِرَ 7

حُبُكِ أُذُنِ رُبُعُ صُحُفِ 8

أَعِظُ تَزِرُ يَرِثُ يَعِدُ 9

Notes for Unit 13

Practice with short vowels

Master this page thoroughly before proceeding.

Refer to Units 7 and 8 or the Alphabet Summary Chart if there is any difficulty recognizing individual letters.

Notice the varying ways in which the vowel 'a' is sounded, for example:

خَلَقَكَ KHa La Qa Ka

Try reading against the clock. If you can read the whole page in three minutes, you are doing well.

هُوَ لَكَ هِىَ بِكَ تَرَ لِمَ مَعَ 1

خَلَقَ وَقَبَ حَسَدَ كَسَبَ قَدَرَ 2

وَهَبَ صَدَقَ شَرَحَ فَرَضَ وَلَدَ 3

قُدِرَ هُدِىَ نُفِخَ خُلِقَ غُفِرَ 4

ضُرِبَ وُعِدَ كُتِبَ يَضَعُ قُضِىَ 5

رَضِىَ سَمِعَ نَسِىَ بَخِلَ غَشِىَ 6

لَبِثَ وَلِىَ لَقِىَ يَدِىَ تَبِعَ 7

لَهُوَ أُخَرَ عُقَدِ أُفُقِ رُسُلُ 8

وَجَدَكَ عَدَلَكَ خَلَقَكَ بِيَدِكَ 9

SECTION THREE

Tanwin, Sukun & Shaddah

Tanwi̲n

Tanwīn means adding an 'n' sound to a vowel 'a', 'i' and 'u'.
Tanwīn only occurs at the end of words.

Tanwi̲n with the vowel 'a'

The extra stroke above the vowel 'a' represents 'n', for example:

دً = Dan (Note: this is not pronounced as the English word 'Dan')

After tanwīn with the vowel 'a', an alif is written but not pronounced when the 'an' is pronounced, as in:

أَبَدًا = 'a Ba Dan

No alif is written after tanwīn with a taa' marbūṭah: ـةً ةً. See line 8.

Also, no alif is written after a hamzah with tanwīn which is preceded by a long vowel, for example:

نِسَآءً = Ni Saaaa 'an

Also, no vertical alif is written after the tanwīn in words like هُدًى - Hu Dan. Instead, a ى without dots follows the tanwin. This ى is called an alif maqṣūrah. (See also, Unit 24.)

Note the position of the alif after the laam, as in رُسُلًا and مَثَلًا .

The best way to understand the pronunciation of tanwīn is to follow the text of the Madīnah Muṣ-ḥaf closely while listening to and imitating a good reciter.

The **fat-ḥah tanwīn** in the Madīnah Muṣ-ḥaf is **written in two ways:**

1 directly above the fat-ḥah: ـً
2 staggered: ـً

Izha̲r (إِظْهَار)

When it is written as ـً (the tanwīn directly above the fat-ḥah), tanwīn is pronounced distinctly, and there is no pausing or humming (*ghunnah*) when pronouncing it. This is when the tanwīn is followed by the throat letters:

ء ح خ ع غ هـ

This short and distinct pronunciation of tanwīn is called **iẓhār**, as in:

نَارًا خَالِدًا

Ghunnah (humming nasal sound)

When the tanwīn is written in a staggered fashion, this indicates that the tanwīn should be pronounced with a humming nasal sound called **ghunnah**.

نَفْسًا زَكِيَّةً

Iqla̲b (إِقْلَاب)

The tanwīn is converted to a small meem (م) and pronounced as an 'm' when the following letter is a baa':

سَمِيعًا بَصِيرًا

This process is iqlāb or conversion.

ءًا بًا تًا ثًا جًا حًا خًا 1

دًا ذًا رًا زًا سًا شًا 2

صًا ضًا طًا ظًا عًا غًا فًا قًا 3

كًا لًا مًا نًا هًا وًا يًا 4

أَبَدًا رَغَدًا طَبَقًا جَنَفًا مَلِكًا 5

مَثَلًا عِنَبًا قَصَصًا جُزْءًا ثَمَنًا 6

أَسِفًا قَدَرًا لَبَنًا كَذِبًا شَطَطًا 7

كُفُوًا رُسُلًا عَلَقَةً بَقَرَةً حَسَنَةً نَخِرَةً 8

نَارًا خَالِدًا نَفْسًا زَكِيَّةً سَمِيعًا بَصِيرًا 9

Tanwīn with the vowel 'i'

An extra stroke below a final vowel 'i' produces an 'n' sound, for example:

دٍ = Din   يَدٍ = Ya Din

The tanwīn with the vowel 'i' in the Madīnah Muṣ-ḥaf is written in two ways:

1 directly below the kasrah, ‗‗ as in: حَاسِدٍ إِذَا

2 staggered, ‗‗ as in: بِخَلْقٍ جَدِيدٍ

Iẓhār (إِظْهَار)

When the tanwīn is written as ‗‗ (directly below the kasrah), it is pronounced distinctly, and there is no pausing or humming (*ghunnah*) when pronouncing it. This is when the tanwīn is followed by the throat letters:

ء ح خ غ ع هـ

This short and distinct pronunciation of the 'n' sound is called **iẓhār**, as in:

يَوْمَئِذٍ عَن   أَمْرٍ حَكِيمٍ   حَاسِدٍ إِذَا

Ghunnah (humming nasal sound)

When the tanwīn is staggered as ‗‗, this indicates that the tanwīn should be pronounced with a nasal sound called ghunnah, while lingering on it, as in:

يَوْمَئِذٍ تُحَدِّثُ   لِنَفْسٍ شَيْئًا   نَاصِيَةٍ كَاذِبَةٍ

The tanwīn is a vowelless Noon. As such, it may also be merged or assimilated into a following letter . For more details of this, see Section Six.

Iqlāb (إِقْلَاب)

The tanwīn is replaced by a small Mīm and pronounced as an 'm' when the following letter is a Bā'. This process is known as iqlāb.

كِرَامٍ بَرَرَةٍ   بِعَذَابٍ بَئِيسٍ   كُلُّ نَفْسٍ بِمَا

ءٍ بٍ تٍ ثٍ جٍ حٍ خٍ 1

دٍ ذٍ رٍ زٍ سٍ شٍ 2

صٍ ضٍ طٍ ظٍ عٍ غٍ فٍ قٍ 3

كٍ لٍ مٍ نٍ هٍـ وٍ يٍ 4

عَمَدٍ طَبَقٍ كَبَدٍ عَلَقٍ مَسَدٍ 5

لَهَبٍ سَنَةٍ نَهَرٍ شَجَرٍ غَضَبٍ 6

سَحَرٍ كَذِبٍ فُرُشٍ خَبَرٍ بِدَمٍ 7

حَرَجٍ أُكُلٍ سَفَرَةٍ بَرَرَةٍ رَقَبَةٍ 8

أَمْرٍ حَكِيمٍ لِنَفْسٍ شَيْـًٔا بِعَذَابٍۭ بَئِيسٍ 9

Notes for Unit 16

Tanwi̱n with the vowel 'u'

An extra hook with a final vowel 'u' produces an 'n' sound, for example:

بٌ = Bun   كِتَـٰبٌ = Ki Taa Bun

(Note: بٌ is not pronounced as the English word 'Bun'.)

The tanwīn with the vowel 'u' in the Madīnah Muṣ-ḥaf is written in two ways:

1. directly above the ḍammah and inverted, ـٌ as in: عَذَابٌ عَظِيمٌ
2. staggered, ـٌ as in: فَصَبْرٌ جَمِيلٌ

Izha̱r (إِظْهَار)

When the tanwīn is written as ـٌ (inverted and above the ḍammah), it is pronounced distinctly, and there is no pausing or humming (*ghunnah*) when pronouncing it. This is when the tanwīn is followed by the throat letters:

ء ح خ ع غ هـ

This short and distinct pronunciation of the 'n' sound is called **iẓhār**, as in:

عَذَابٌ عَظِيمٌ   نَارٌ حَامِيَةٌ   سَلَـٰمٌ هِىَ

Ghunnah (humming nasal sound)

When the tanwīn is staggered as ـٌ, this shows that the tanwīn should be pronounced with a nasal sound called ghunnah, while lingering on it, as in:

عَذَابٌ قَرِيبٌ   جَنَّـٰتٌ تَجْرِى   فَصَبْرٌ جَمِيلٌ

The tanwīn is a vowelless نْ. As such, it may also be merged or assimilated into a following letter . For more details of this, see Units 39-40.

Iqla̱b (إِقْلَاب)

The tanwīn is replaced by a small Mīm and pronounced as an 'm' when the following letter is a Bā'. This process is known as iqlāb or conversion.

صُمٌّ بُكْمٌ عُمْىٌ   كَافِرٌ بِهِ   عَلِيمٌ بِذَاتِ

ءٌ بٌ تٌ ثٌ جٌ حٌ خٌ 1

دٌ ذٌ رٌ زٌ سٌ شٌ 2

صٌ ضٌ طٌ ظٌ عٌ غٌ فٌ قٌ 3

كٌ لٌ مٌ نٌ هـٌ وٌ ىٌ 4

سُرُرٌ أُذُنٌ كُتُبٌ رُسُلٌ رَجُلٌ 5

جُدَدٌ أَحَدٌ قَسَمٌ بَشَرٌ سِنَةٌ 6

مَرَضٌ حَرَجٌ لَعِبٌ حُمُرٌ وَلَدٌ 7

غَبَرَةٌ قَتَرَةٌ بَقَرَةٌ عَذَابٌ عَظِيمٌ 8

فَصَبْرٌ جَمِيلٌ صُمٌّ بُكْمٌ عُمْىٌ 9

Notes for Unit 17

The sukun

A sukūn is a symbol like the head of a small ḥaa' (ـْـ) above a letter .
(In modern Arabic, it is written as a complete circle.)

A letter with a sukūn has no vowel of its own. Such a letter is therefore called a **vowelless letter.**

The function of a sukūn is to join in pronunciation the letter over which it occurs to the previous letter and vowel to form one syllable.

لَ	La	يَغْفِرْ	Yagh fir
لَمْ	Lam	يُدْخِلْكُمْ	Yud khil kum

Qalqalah

When a sukūn occurs on any of the five letters (*read from right to left*):

ق ط ب ج د

- these letters are given an added stress especially if they occur at the end of an utterance. This is to prevent these letters from being mistaken in pronunciation for another:

ق for a ك or ء	ج for a ش
ط for a ت	د for a ت
ب for a م	

Pronouncing these letters with an added stress is called qalqalah, meaning 'shakiness'. For examples, see the words in line 9 opposite, each of which ends with a qalqalah letter.

The qalqalah letters are the ones in the two words: قُطْبُ جَدْ .

1 أَنْ إِذْ أَمْ إِنْ بَلْ تُبْ خُذْ دَعْ

2 ذَرْ ذُقْ زِدْ سَلْ فَصُرْ عَنْ عِدْ

3 وَعِظْ قَدْ قُلْ قُمْ كَمْ لَكُمْ كُنْ كُلْ

4 لَمْ لَنْ مَنْ مِنْ هَبْ لِى فَهَلْ لَهُمْ

5 أَنزِلْ أَمْهِلْ أَلْقَتْ ٱذْهَبْ ٱدْفَعْ

6 أَتِمْ أَمْسِكْ أَحْسِنْ ٱصْبِرْ ٱرْكُضْ

7 يُعْظِمْ أَقْتُلْ يَغْفِرْ تَسْمَعْ يُدْخِلْكُمْ

8 نَقْصُصْ زِلْتُمْ قُلْتُمْ لَكُنتُمْ طِبْتُمْ

9 ذُقْ نَسْقُطْ كَسَبْ أَخْرُجْ يُولَدْ

Notes for Unit 18

Sukun on a waw preceded by a vowel 'a'

A Sukūn on a wāw preceded by a letter with a vowel 'a' produces the sound of 'aw', sounded as '*ow*' in the English word '*now*', for example:

نَوْ = NaW (pronounced 'now')

نَوْمٌ = Naw Mun

كَوْثَرَ = Kaw THa Ra

The 'aw' sound is called a 'diphthong' or a 'vowel glide' because it starts off with the sound of the vowel 'a' and ends with the sound of the vowel 'u'.

أَوْ بَوْ تَوْ ثَوْ جَوْ حَوْ خَوْ 1

دَوْ ذَوْ رَوْ زَوْ سَوْ شَوْ 2

صَوْ ضَوْ طَوْ ظَوْ عَوْ غَوْ فَوْ قَوْ 3

كَوْ لَوْ مَوْ نَوْ هَوْ وَوْ يَوْ 4

أَوْهَنَ تَوْبَةً جَوْفٍ خَوْفٍ رَوْحٌ 5

زَوْجًا سَوْفَ صَوْمًا غَوْرًا فَوْتَ 6

قَوْلَ كَوْثَرَ لَوْمَةَ نَوْمٌ هَوْنًا 7

يَوْمَ سَوْطَ صَوْتَ لَوْحٍ يَوْمَئِذٍ 8

وَإِنَّ أَوْهَنَ ٱلْبُيُوتِ لَبَيْتُ ٱلْعَنكَبُوتِ 9

Notes for Unit 19

Sukun on a ya' preceded by a vowel 'a'

Sukūn on a yaa' preceded by a letter with a vowel 'a' produces the sound of 'ay' which is pronounced somewhat like the 'i' in *site*, for example:

بَيْ = Bay (quite distinct from the English word 'bay')

بَيْتِ = Bay Ti

The 'ay' sound is called a 'diphthong' or a 'vowel glide' because it starts off with the sound of the vowel 'a' and ends with the sound of the vowel 'i'.

أَيْ بَيْ تَيْ ثَيْ جَيْ حَيْ خَيْ دَيْ 1

ذَيْ رَيْ زَيْ سَيْ شَيْ صَيْ ضَيْ 2

طَيْ ظَيْ عَيْ غَيْ فَيْ قَيْ كَيْ 3

لَيْ مَيْ نَيْ هَيْ وَيْ يَيْ 4

أَيْنَ بَيْتِ حَيْثُ خَيْرٌ بِدَيْنٍ 5

قُرَيْشٍ زَيْغٌ شَيْءٌ صَيْفِ ضَيْفِ 6

طَيْرًا عَيْنٌ غَيْرَ كَيْدًا لَيْتَ مَيْتًا 7

وَيْلٌ هَيْتَ ضَيْقٍ رَيْبَ لَيْسَ 8

ذَٰلِكَ ٱلْكِتَـٰبُ لَا رَيْبَ فِيهِ 9

Notes for Unit 20

The Hamzah with a suk<u>u</u>n

A sukūn on a hamzah above an Alif, a Yā' (without dots) or a Wāw produces an abrupt, jerky sound after the short vowels a, i and u.
Take care not to lengthen these vowels. For example:

شَأْنٌ = Sha' Nun

يُؤْمِنُ = Yu' Mi Nu

جِئْتِ = Ji' Ti

(The hamzah is transliterated into English as a closed inverted comma.)

1 مُؤْصَدَةٌ شَأْنٌ يَأْمُرُكُمْ يُـؤْمِنُ

2 تُؤْمَرُونَ تَأْكُلُونَ يُـؤْتُونَ يُـؤْفَكُونَ

3 يَأْتِكُمْ وَأْمُرْ تَأْتِيهِمْ مَأْوَاهُمْ كَأْسًا

4 يَأْبَ نَأْتِ قَرَأْتِ بَأْسٍ مَأْكُولٍ

5 أَحْمَدُ يَسْأَلُ قُرِئَ أَأَنتَ ءَإِلَـٰهٌ

6 شَيْـًٔا لُؤْلُؤًا إِبْرَٰهِيمَ إِبْرَٰهِـۧمَ

7 يَوْمَئِذٍ أُكُلٍ لُؤْلُؤٌ شَىْءٌ نَبَإِىْ نَبَإٍ

8 يَـٰٓأَبَتِ ٱفْعَلْ مَا تُؤْمَرُ

9 سَتَجِدُنِىٓ إِن شَآءَ ٱللَّهُ مِنَ ٱلصَّـٰبِرِينَ

Notes for Unit 21

The Shaddah

A shaddah is a small ـّـ sign placed above a letter.

The shaddah joins and doubles:

1 It joins in pronunciation the letter above which it occurs to the preceding letter and vowel.
2 The letter above which it occurs is then repeated and pronounced with its own vowel.

رَبَّ = Rab Ba, pronounced with a distinct stress on the B.
Notice that the English translation has two 'B's whereas in the Arabic, because of the shaddah, only one Baa' is needed.

Distinguish between:

نَزَلَ = na za la   نَزَّلَ = naz za la

The effect of the shaddah, which comes from a word meaning 'to strengthen' or 'to intensify' is to place a strong emphasis on the letter it doubles.

Ghunnah with a mim and nun having a shadddah

A **mīm** or **nūn** with a shaddah is pronounced with a pleasant humming sound called *ghunnah*.
You linger on or hum this **mīm** or **nūn** for about two beats or *harakahs* - that is, about twice as long as a short vowel.

مِمَّ = Mimm-ma   إِنَّ = Inn-na

مِمَّا = Mimm-maa   إِنَّا = Inn-naa

ثُمَّ = Thumm-ma   أَنَّ = Ann-na

رَبْ بَ=رَبَّ إِنْ نَ=إِنَّ ثُمْ مَ=ثُمَّ 1

عَمَّ ثُمَّ مَنَّ مَدَّ قَلَّ حَجَّ أَنَّ 2

تَبَّ ظَنَّ صَبَّ مِمَّ أَيِّ شَرِّ صَلِّ كُلُّ 3

حُبًّا جَمًّا دَكًّا شَقًّا صَفًّا حَقٌّ حَلٌّ 4

أُمٌّ كُلٌّ رَبٌّ غَمٍّ غِلٍّ ظِلٍّ ضُرٍّ 5

صَدَّقَ قَدَّرَ كَذَّبَ وَدَّعَكَ عَلَّمَ 6

حُصِّلَ مِلَّةَ تَبَّتْ هَمَّتْ قُوَّةَ سُيِّرَتْ 7

تَقَبَّلَ كَذَّبَتْ عُطِّلَتْ فَسَنُيَسِّرُهُ 8

لَا عِلْمَ لَنَآ إِلَّا مَا عَلَّمْتَنَا 9

SECTION FOUR

Long Vowels

Notes for Unit 22

Long vowels

An Alif lengthens the vowel 'a'

A bare alif - that is, an alif without a hamzah, a vowel or a sukūn, is used to lengthen the vowel 'a'.

بَ = Ba; بَا = Baa

The vowel thus lengthened is twice the length of the short vowel in pronunciation.

بَا may be transliterated as Baa or Bā. In transliteration into English, a stroke or bar above a vowel, indicates a long vowel.

Laam, hamza, alif

In line 9, notice the position of the hamzah with the vowel 'a' (ءَ) in the 2nd, 4th and last word: the hamzah appears <u>before</u> the alif, and not <u>on</u> the alif. The alif therefore lengthens the vowel 'a' on the hamzah.

For example:

In the word لِأَدَمَ, the first three letters are laam, hamzah and then alif. The word is pronounced **li 'aa dama**.

In لَأَيَةً the first three letters are laam, hamzah, and then alif. The word is pronounced **la 'aa ya tan.**

Other such words in the Madīnah Muṣ-ḥaf are:

ٱلْأَخِرِ ٱلْأَخِرَةِ ٱلْأَصَالِ

ءَا بَا تَا ثَا جَا حَا خَا 1

دَا ذَا رَا زَا سَا شَا 2

صَا ضَا طَا ظَا عَا غَا فَا قَا 3

كَا لَا مَا نَا هَا وَا يَا 4

ذَاتَ خَافَ كَانَ قَالَ رَانَ تَابَ 5

عَادَ نَارًا هَادٍ خِطَابًا عَامٍ ثَوَابًا 6

أَفَاقَ يَخَافُ أَصَابَ جُنَاحَ كَوَاعِبَ 7

جَاعِلٌ حَافِظٌ خَالِدًا مُطَاعٍ غَاسِقٍ 8

ءَادَمَ لِأَدَمَ ءَايَةً لَأَيَـةً ءَاخِرِ وَلَلْأَخِرَةُ 9

Notes for Unit 23

Long vowels

The suspended Alif

A small suspended alif after a vowel ‘a’ also lengthens the vowel ‘a’, as in:

إِلَٰهَ = i Laa Ha

كِتَٰبٌ = Ki Taa Bun

كِتَٰبٌ is pronounced exactly as كِتَابٌ .

ءَٰ بَـٰ تَـٰ ثَـٰ جَـٰ حَـٰ خَـٰ دَٰ ذَٰ 1

رَٰ زَٰ سَـٰ شَـٰ صَـٰ ضَـٰ طَـٰ ظَـٰ عَـٰ 2

غَـٰ فَـٰ قَـٰ كَـٰ لَـٰ مَـٰ نَـٰ هَـٰ وَٰ يَـٰ 3

إِلَـٰهَ كِتَـٰبٌ رَحْمَـٰنُ مُبَـٰرَكَةٍ تَبَارَكَ تَابَ 4

نَفَّـٰثَـٰتِ تِـجَـٰرَتُهُمْ سُبْحَـٰنَكَ خَـٰلِدُونَ رَانَ 5

كِذَّٰبًا صِرَٰطَ إِنسَـٰنُ صَـٰلِحَـٰتِ شَيْطَـٰنِ 6

عِظَـٰمًا عَـٰدِيَـٰتِ قَـٰنِتَـٰتٍ سَلَـٰمٌ سَمَـٰوَٰتِ 7

رَزَقْنَـٰهُمْ كَـٰفِرِينَ هَـٰذَا هَـٰذِهِ هَـٰٓؤُلَآءِ 8

مُسْلِمَـٰتٍ مُؤْمِنَـٰتٍ قَـٰنِتَـٰتٍ تَـٰٓئِبَـٰتٍ عَـٰبِدَٰتٍ 9

Notes for Unit 24

Long vowels

The Alif Maqsurah

An Alif Maqṣūrah is an alif written as ى when it appears at the end of certain words.The Alif Maqṣūrah lengthens the vowel 'a':

يَغْشَىٰ is pronounced *yagh shaa.*

Notice the small suspended alif above the alif maqṣūrah, written as ىٰ. When it appears joined to a following letter, or joined to a previous and following letter, the alif maqṣūrah is written as a shortened yā' without dots:

تَقْوَىٰهَا is pronounced *taq waa haa*

ضُحَىٰهَا is pronounced *ḍu ḥaa haa*

The words in lines 1 - 3 are from Sūrah al-Layl (sūrah 92) which has many examples of alif maqṣūrah as ى.

The words in lines 5 - 6 are from Sūrah ash-Shams (sūrah 91) which has many examples of the alif maqṣūrah within a word.

When the alif maqṣūrah is followed by a hamzatu-l waṣl, it is written without the suspended alif, as in:

عِيسَى ٱبْنُ مَرْيَمَ

Silent waw

In line 7, a suspended alif appears on a wāw: وٰ . This wāw remains silent but the suspended alif lengthens the vowel 'a':

زَكَوٰةٍ is pronounced *za kaa tin.*

Other words like this are:

صَلَوٰةً *ṣa laa tan*

حَيَوٰةِ *ḥa yaa ti*

Silent alif

In line 8, the first two words have an alif with a small circle: ا۠. This ا۠ always remains silent.

Pausal alif

In line 8, a small oval shape appears above the final alif in أَنَا۠ . This does not lengthen the vowel 'a':

أَنَا۠ is pronounced *a-na*, not *a-naa.*

However when أَنَا۠ appears at the end of an utterance it is pronounced *a-naa.*

1 يَغۡشَىٰ تَـجَلَّىٰ أُنثَىٰ شَتَّىٰ أَعۡطَىٰ

2 وَٱتَّقَىٰ حُسۡنَىٰ يُسۡرَىٰ عُسۡرَىٰ

3 تَرَدَّىٰ هُدَىٰ أُولَىٰ تَلَظَّىٰ يَتَزَكَّىٰ

4 أَشۡقَى ٱلَّذِى أَتۡقَى ٱلَّذِى عِيسَى ٱبۡنُ مَرۡيَمَ

5 ضُحَىٰهَا تَلَىٰهَا جَلَّىٰهَا سَوَّىٰهَا تَقۡوَىٰهَا

6 زَكَّىٰهَا دَسَّىٰهَا بِطَغۡوَىٰهَا أَشۡقَىٰهَا

7 حَيَوٰةُ زَكَوٰةَ مَنَوٰةَ كَمِشۡكَوٰةٍ

8 أُوْلُواْ قُولُواْ أَنَاْ بَشَرٌ

9 قَدۡ أَفۡلَحَ مَن زَكَّىٰهَا وَ قَدۡ خَابَ مَن دَسَّىٰهَا

Notes for Unit 25

Long vowels

A Yaa' lengthens the vowel 'i'

The bare letter ى - that is, a Yaa' without a vowel or sukūn, is used to lengthen the vowel i:

بِ = Bi (short)

بِى = Biy (long), sounded as *'bee'* in *beef*.

This may be transliterated as *Bii*, *Bee*, or *Bī*. In transliteration into English, a stroke or bar above a vowel indicates a long vowel.

يَتِيمًا = Ya Tiy Man, or Ya Tī Man

(sounded as *Ya Tee Man*).

A Yaa' with a shaddah, preceded by a vowel 'i', lengthens the vowel 'i'. The Yaa' is then repeated with its own vowel, as in:

نَبِيُّهُمْ = Na Biy Yu Hum

(pronounced *Na Bee Yu Hum*).

A small Yaa'

A small Yaa', written as (ـے) after a final vowel 'i' also lengthens the vowel 'i' - about twice the length of the short vowel - as in:

بِهِۦ = Bi Hiy, pronounced *Bi Hee*

Sometimes a wavy sign (~) called a **maddah** is placed above the small Yaa' - this lengthens the vowel 'i' about four times the length of the short vowel.

بِهِۦٓ = Bi Hiiiy, pronounced *Bi Heeee*

The Yaa' has a maddah when the following letter is a hamzah:

وَأَمْرِهِۦٓ إِلَىٰ بِهِۦٓ أَن

إِى بِى تِى ثِى جِى حِى خِى 1

دِى ذِى رِى زِى سِى شِى 2

صِى ضِى طِى ظِى عِى غِى فِى 3

قِى كِى لِى مِى نِى هِى وِى يِى 4

مُبِينٍ يَتِيمًا كَثِيرًا مَجِيدٌ مُحِيطٌ 5

أَخِيهِ دِينِ نَذِيرٌ كَرِيمٍ تَـجْزِى 6

يَسِيرًا يَمْشِى بَصِيرًا لَطِيفٌ عَظِيمٌ 7

عِينٌ غِيضَ قِيلَ أَكِيدُ عَلِيمٌ 8

مِيقَاتًا بَنِيهِ شَهِيدٌ نَبِيُّهُم بِهِۦ لِرَبِّهِۦ 9

Notes for Unit 26

Long vowels

A Waw lengthens the vowel 'u'

The bare letter و - that is, a wāw without a vowel or a sukūn, is used to lengthen the vowel *u*:

بُ = Bu

بُو = Buw, pronounced '*boo*' as in the English word '*boot*'; may be transliterated as Bū.

A wāw with a shaddah, preceded by a vowel 'u', lengthens the vowel 'u' . The wāw is then repeated with its own vowel, as in:

ثُوِّبَ = thuw wi ba (pronounced *thoo wi ba*)

A small Waw

A small wāw after a final vowel 'u' also lengthens the vowel 'u' - about twice the length of the short vowel - as in:

إِنَّهُۥ = in na huw (pronounced *'in na hoo*).

Sometimes a wavy sign called a **maddah** is placed above the small wāw - this lengthens the vowel 'u' about four times the length of the short vowel.

أَمْرُهُۥٓ = am ru huw (pronounced *'am ru hoooo*).

مَالُهُۥٓ = maa lu huw (pronounced *maa lu hoooo*).

The small wāw has a maddah when the following letter is a hamzah, whether the hamzah is written on its own or with an alif.

أُو بُو تُو ثُو جُو حُو خُو 1

دُو ذُو رُو زُو سُو شُو 2

صُو ضُو طُو ظُو عُو غُو فُو 3

قُو كُو لُو مُو نُو هُو وُو يُو 4

أُوتِىَ بُورِكَ تُورُونَ ثُوِّبَ وُجُوهٌ حُورٌ 5

دُولَةً لَذُو زُورًا يَصُومُونَ صُورِ 6

طُورِ أَعُوذُ تَفُورُ يَقُولُونَ تَكُونُ 7

مَوْقُوفُونَ نُوحٌ صَابِئُونَ سَاهُونَ 8

زَيْتُونٍ قُلُوبٌ كُوِّرَتْ رِبِّيُّونَ إِنَّهُۥ 9

Notes for Unit 27

Practice with short and long vowels

In lines 1 - 4, some reading exercises show the importance of keeping short vowels short and lengthening long vowels.

For example:

كَانَ means *he was*

كَانَا means *they both were*

إِنَّ means *surely*

إِنَّا means *surely we.*

Distinguishing between similar sounds

In lines 5 - 8, reading exercises show the importance of distinguishing between similar but different sounds. If you are not careful, you could be saying something totally different from what is intended. The meanings will show this:

Line 5: painful, knowing; fig, clay; meeting, divorce

Line 6: sin, name, with defences; sinner, defender

Line7: fleeing, with war; good, other; after, some

Line 8: we humbled them, we provided shade; determination, bone

Line 9: heart, dog; they said, they measured out to them.

1 عَمَّ عَمَّا فِيمَ فِيمَا مِمَّ مِـمَّا

2 كَانَ كَانَا إِنَّ إِنَّا ظَنَّ ظَنَّا

3 تَابَا قَالَا كَلَّا لِيَكُونَا فَقُولَا رَسُولَا

4 ٱذْهَبَا شِئْتُمَا فَلَاتَقْرَبَا أَطَاعُونَا

5 أَلِيمٌ عَلِيمٌ تِينٍ طِينٍ ٱلتَّلَاقِ ٱلطَّلَاقُ

6 إِثْمَ ٱسْمُ بِعِصَمِ ءَاثِمٌ عَاصِمٍ

7 هَرَبًا بِحَرْبٍ خَيْرٍ غَيْرَ بَعْدُ بَعْضُ

8 ذَلَّلْنَٰهَا ظَلَّلْنَا ٱلْعَزْمِ ٱلْعَظْمُ

9 ٱلْقَلْبِ ٱلْكَلْبِ قَالُوا۟ كَالُوهُمْ

Notes for Unit 28

Reading practice

Reading practice on this page is meant to consolidate rules and sounds covered on previous pages.

Repeat this page as many times as necessary to improve both accuracy and speed.

قَوْمِى أَيْدِى رُوحِى دِينِى ضَيْفِى 1

تَدْعُو يَرْجُو تَتْلُو نَبْلُوكُمْ يَعْفُو 2

أَنتَ لَسْتَ بَطْشَ بَعْدُ نَحْنُ 3

أَخْرَجَ أَغْطَشَ أَرْسَلَ لَهُمْ رَفَعْنَا 4

يَحْسَبُ يُوَسْوِسُ نَعْبُدُ فَرَغْتَ 5

ٱلْحَمْدُ أَنْعَمْتَ أَعْطَيْنَـٰكَ أَنزَلْنَـٰهُ 6

يَشْهَدُ تَرْهَقُ تَعْرِفُ أُقْسِمُ يَشْرَبُ 7

نُصِبَتْ سُطِحَتْ أَثَرْنَ وَسَطْنَ بِإِذْنِ 8

سَيَعْلَمُونَ يَسْتَوْفُونَ يَنظُرُونَ تَنظُرُونَ 9

Notes for Unit 29

Reading practice

Reading practice on this page is meant to consolidate rules and sounds covered on previous pages.

Repeat this page as many times as necessary to improve both accuracy and speed.

1 أَجْرُ حَبْلٌ فَصْلُ عَدْنٍ خُسْرٍ

2 مَسْغَبَةٍ مَتْرَبَةٍ مَقْرَبَةٍ تَضْلِيلٍ تَقْوِيمٍ

3 تَكْذِيبٍ صِدْقٍ مَرْفُوعَةٍ مَمْنُوعَةٍ

4 مَشْهُودٍ مَجْنُونٍ قَدْحًا نَقْعًا صُبْحًا

5 أَلْبَابًا أَشْتَاتًا أَعْنَابًا أَتْرَابًا أَفْوَاجًا

6 يَمُدُّ يَدُعُّ يَظُنُّ يَحُضُّ يَفِرُّ

7 يُكَذِّبُ تُحَدِّثُ نُيَسِّرُ نُقَدِّسُ

8 يَخْتَصُّ يُبَيِّنُ مُتُّمْ بِأَنَّهُمْ مُصَلِّينَ

9 مُتَّقِينَ مُنفَكِّينَ خَفَّتْ مُدَّتْ حُقَّتْ

Notes for Unit 30

Reading practice

Reading practice on this page is meant to consolidate rules and sounds covered on previous pages.

Repeat this page as many times as necessary to improve both accuracy and speed.

Observe ***ghunnah*** (humming and lingering) on the Mīm and Nūn having a shaddah:

فَلَمَّا = *fa lamm̲ maa*

إِنَّمَا = *Inn̲ na maa*

أَلَّا بَلَّا كَلَّا إِلَّا إِيَّاكَ مِنَّا إِنَّا 1

عَنِّى مِنِّى إِنِّى رَبِّى أَنِّى 2

جَلَّىٰهَا زَكَّىٰهَا عُقْبَـٰهَا أَنَاسِىَّ 3

ٱللَّهُ رَبُّنَا فَلَمَّا إِنَّمَا أَيُّهَا يُقَدِّرُ 4

أَمَّا كُنَّا إِنَّهَا لَعَلَّ فِيهِنَّ ثُمَّ 5

كَرَّةٌ قَيِّمَةٌ عَشِيَّةً عِلِّيِّينَ 6

وَمَآ ءَاتَىٰكُمُ ٱلرَّسُولُ فَخُذُوهُ 7

وَمَا نَهَىٰكُمْ عَنْهُ فَٱنتَهُوا۟ 8

وَإِذْ قَالَ إِبْرَٰهِيمُ لِأَبِيهِ ءَازَرَ فَصَلِّ لِرَبِّكَ وَٱنْحَرْ 9

Notes for Unit 31

The maddah

A wavy sign, called ***maddah***, is placed over a long vowelled letter, to prolong the vowel. A vowel may be lengthened two, four or six lengths or *ḥarakahs*. Prolonging a vowel to a required length is a rough practice based on estimation. As a guide, move the thumb while pronouncing the vowel so that it touches the tips of the same number of fingers.

To prolong the vowel *a* of *Baa* to four ḥarakahs, say *Ba* and at the same time move your thumb so that it touches the tips of the other fingers from the index finger to the little finger. This will produce a long vowel of four ḥarakahs. To produce a long vowel of six ḥarakahs, move the thumb back and stop at the tip of the middle finger.

Maddah before hamzah

When immediately followed by a hamzah, a vowel is lengthened to four ḥarakahs.

This maddah is obligatory when the hamzah belongs to the same word.

جَآءَ = *Jaaaa'a*

سُوٓءِ = *Suuuu 'i*

جِيٓءَ = *Jiiii 'a*

When the hamzah is the first letter of the following word, the vowel with the maddah may be lengthened to four ḥarakahs also. Or, it could be limited to two ḥarakahs. In reciting, you could adopt either of these but stick to the one you choose consistently.

بِمَآ أُنزِلَ = *Bi maa 'unn zi la*
or *Bi maaaa 'unn zi la.*

Notice the vowelless nūn in أُنزِلَ . Observe ghunnah when pronouncing it.

بَا بُو بِى   بَآ بُوٓ بِىٓ 1

سَا سُو سِى   سَآ سُوٓ سِىٓ 2

بَآءَ جَآءَ سَآءَ شَآءَ مَآءَهَا سُوٓءِ 3

عَطَآءً غُثَآءً نِسَآءً أَدَآءً سَوَآءٌ جَزَآءٌ 4

بَلَآءٌ دِمَآءُكُمْ حُنَفَآءَ وَرَآءَهُ أَوْلِيَآءُ 5

جِىٓءَ سِىٓءَ يُضِىٓءُ بَرِىٓءٌ خَطِيٓـَٔتُهُ 6

مَلَٰٓئِكَةُ يَٰٓـَٔادَمُ كَبَٰٓئِرَ لَآ إِلَٰهَ إِلَّآ أَنتَ 7

جَآءُوكَ ءَالَآءِ ءَآلْـَٔنَ بَآءُو 8

هَٰٓأَنتُمْ يَٰٓأَيُّهَا يَٰٓأَيَّتُهَا يَٰٓإِبْرَٰهِيمُ 9

Notes for Unit 32

Maddah followed by a suku̱n or shaddah

When there is a maddah followed by a letter with a sukūn or shaddah, the vowel has to be prolonged to six ḥarakahs.

وَلَا ٱلضَّآلِّينَ = *wa laḍ ḍaaaaaal leen*

Pausing on a final consonant
In pausing on a final consonant preceded by a long vowel, the long vowel may be prolonged to four or six ḥarakahs long:

غَفُور = *ghafuuuur* or *ghafuuuuuur*

رَحِيم = *rahiiiim* or *rahiiiiiim*

نَاس = *naaaas* or *naaaaaas*

Muqaṭṭa'āt or Single Letters

Certain Sūrahs in the Qur'ān begin with independent letters. Such letters, even when attached to each other, must be pronounced separately as they are pronounced while reading the alphabet. There are 14 such letters.

1. The letter alif as in الٓر, is pronounced as alif. It has no vowels.
2. The letters ح ر ط ه ى appear without any vowel.
Each of these letters is pronounced as if it has a long vowel 'a' - two ḥarakahs:
e.g. طه = ṭaa haa
3. The remaining letters
نٓ مٓ لٓ كٓ قٓ عٓ صٓ سٓ
all carry a maddah and are lengthened to six ḥarakahs, e.g. عٓسٓقٓ.

ضَآلًّا حَآجَّك دَآبَّةً لَرَآدُّك خَآصَّةً 1

كَآفَّةً بِضَآرِّهِمْ تَحَآضُّونَ جَآنٌّ 2

ءَآمِّينَ ظَآنِّينَ 3

الٓمٓ الٓمٓصٓ الٓر الٓمٓر كٓهيعٓصٓ 4

طه طسٓمٓ يسٓ صٓ 5

حمٓ عٓسٓقٓ قٓ نٓ 6

SECTION FIVE

The Definite Article
Special Signs & Fine Points

Notes for Unit 33

The hamzatu-l wasl

The hamzatu-l waṣl (the connecting hamzah) is written on an alif as a small ṣaad: ٱ . This is an abbreviation of the word وَصَل which means 'connecting'. A hamzatu-l waṣl is used only above an alif.

A ٱ is disregarded in pronunciation when it does not occur at the beginning of an utterance.

So, ignore the hamzatu-l waṣl when it is preceded by a vowel which is pronounced and followed by a letter with a sukūn or shaddah, as in:

وَٱنْحَرْ = *wa-n ḥar* (the ٱ is ignored completely).

يَومِ ٱلدِّينِ = *yawmi-d dīni* (the alif with the hamzatu-l waṣl and the laam are ignored completely).

In fact, ignore all the intervening letters between the vowel that is pronounced and the letter with a sukūn or a shaddah.

هَـٰذَا ٱلْبَيْتِ = *haadha-l bayti* (the bare alif after the dhaal and the alif with the hamzatu-l waṣl are ignored).

The problem for the beginner arises when a hamzatu-l waṣl appears at the beginning of an utterance. Do you pronounce the ٱ as أَ , إِ or أُ ?

The following rules will help:

RULE ONE

If ٱ is followed by ل , it is usually pronounced as أَ . This is the case if the ٱ is part of the definite article ٱلـ , the relative pronouns ٱلَّذِي ٱلَّذِينَ , and ٱلَّتِي and the words ٱللَّهُمَّ and ٱللَّهُ .

RULE TWO

If ٱ is not followed by ل , and if the first vowel after the ٱ is a fat-ḥah or a kasrah, read the ٱ as إِ :

ٱقْرَأْ is read إِقْرَأْ ; ٱهْدِ is read إِهْدِ

RULE THREE

If the first vowel after the ٱ is a ḍammah, read the ٱ as أُ :

ٱذْكُرْ is read أُذْكُرْ .

• There are some exceptions to these rules, for example:

ٱبْنُ is read إِبْنُ ; ٱسْمُهُ is read إِسْمُهُ.
However, such words do not occur in the Qur'ān at the beginning of an utterance, so the ٱ is ignored in pronunciation, as in: عِيسَى ٱبْنُ

يَوۡمِ ٱلدِّينِ صِرَٰطَ ٱلَّذِينَ غَيۡرِ ٱلۡمَغۡضُوبِ 1

رَبَّ هَٰذَا ٱلۡبَيۡتِ يُرۡبِى ٱلصَّدَقَٰتِ 2

ٱللَّهُ ٱللَّهُمَّ ٱلۡحَمۡدُ ٱلۡمَلِكُ ٱلۡقُدُّوسُ 3

ٱلَّذِىٓ أَطۡعَمَهُمۡ ٱلَّذِينَ هُمۡ ٱلَّذِى ٱلَّتِى 4

ٱقۡرَأۡ ٱذۡهَبۡ ٱفۡعَلُواْ 5

ٱهۡدِ ٱهۡبِطُواْ ٱصۡبِرُواْ 6

ٱذۡكُرُواْ ٱسۡجُدُواْ ٱقۡتُلُواْ ٱرۡكُضۡ 7

وَٱصۡبِرۡ وَٱعۡلَمُواْ ذِى ٱلۡأَوۡتَادِ 8

ذَا ٱلۡجَلَٰلِ ذُو ٱلۡعَرۡشِ وَعَمِلُواْ ٱلصَّٰلِحَٰتِ 9

Notes for Unit 34

Words with the Definite Article - ٱلْـ (al, meaning *'the'*)

The Arabic alphabet is divided into 'sun' (shamsī) and 'moon' (qamarī) letters. The 'sun' letters are:

ت ث د ذ ر ز س ش

ص ض ط ظ ل ن

They are called 'sun' letters because the word for sun شَمْس begins with a ش which is a 'sun' letter.

The remaining letters are 'moon' letters. They are called 'moon' letters because the word for moon قَمَر begins with a ق which is a 'moon' letter.

The writing and pronunciation of ٱلْ and the word it is attached to are affected by whether this word begins with a 'moon' letter or a 'sun' letter.

1. With 'moon' letters

The word ٱلْحَمْدُ begins with ٱلْ, and is followed by the letter Ḥaa' which is a 'moon letter'. The laam keeps its sukūn because the following letter is a 'moon' letter. The words in lines 2 - 4 all begin with a 'moon' letter.

2. With 'sun' letters

When a word is defined by ٱلْـ and begins with a 'sun' letter, the laam loses its sukūn and is not pronounced. The 'sun' letter is then written with a shaddah. (See lines 5 - 7 opposite.) ٱلرَّحْمَٰنُ is thus read: *ar-raḥmānu.*

Stated another way:
If the laam of ٱلْـ has a sukūn, the following letter must be a 'moon' letter. If the laam of ٱلـ is bare (i.e. with no sukūn), the following letter must be a 'sun' letter. (This is all for ease in pronunciation.)

The definite article ٱلْـ is written but dropped in pronunciation when:

1 it is in the middle of an utterance and
2 the following word begins with a sun letter, e.g. هُوَ ٱلرَّحْمَٰنُ

See line 8 opposite for more examples.

The preposition (بِـ - *with*) is attached to the alif of the definite article. The alif is then dropped in pronunciation:

بِـٱلْهُدَىٰ is pronounced *'bil hudā'*.

When the preposition لِـ is joined to the definite article, the hamzatu-l waṣl is dropped in both writing and pronunciation: لِ + ٱلْقَمَرِ = لِلْقَمَرِ

لِ + ٱلرِّجَالِ = لِلرِّجَالِ

See line 9 opposite for more examples.

وَٱلشَّمْسِ وَضُحَىٰهَا وَٱلْقَمَرِ إِذَا تَلَىٰهَا 1

ٱلْأَوَّلُ ٱلْآخِرُ ٱلْبَابُ ٱلْجَمَلُ ٱلْحَمْدُ 2

ٱلْخَوْفُ ٱلْعَظِيمُ ٱلْغَفُورُ ٱلْفَتَّاحُ ٱلْقَدِيرُ 3

ٱلْكَرِيمُ ٱلْمَلِكُ ٱلْهُدَى ٱلْوَدُودُ ٱلْيَمِينُ 4

ٱلتَّوَّابُ ٱلثَّوَابُ ٱلدَّارُ ٱلذِّكْرُ ٱلرَّحْمَٰنُ 5

ٱلزَّيْتُونِ ٱلسَّمَٰوَٰتِ ٱلشَّمْسِ ٱلصَّلَوٰةُ 6

ٱلضَّلَٰلُ ٱلطُّورِ ٱلظِّلُّ ٱلَّيْلِ ٱلنَّاسِ 7

هُوَ ٱلرَّحْمَٰنُ بِـٱلنَّاسِ أَقِمِ ٱلصَّلَوٰةَ 8

لِلرِّجَالِ لِلنِّسَآءِ لِلرَّحْمَٰنِ لِلظَّٰلِمِينَ 9

Notes for Unit 35

Pronunciation of the words Allāh and Allāhumma

The vowel ‘a’ in لَ is normally pronounced as the *‘a’* in *cat*.

However, the لّ with a shaddah in the word ٱللَّهُ is pronounced as ‘lau’ (a rounded sound) when it is preceded by a fat-ḥah or a ḍammah (the vowel ‘a’ or ‘u’). The rounded ‘lau’ is lengthened:

ٱللَّهُ Al laau hu

هُوَ ٱللَّهُ hu wal laau hu

كِتَـٰبُ ٱللَّهِ ki taa bul laau hi

The same applies to:

ٱللَّهُمَّ Al laau hum ma, meaning ‘O Allah’.

However, if the word Allāh or Allāhumma is immediately preceded by a kasrah (the vowel ‘i’), then the لـ is pronounced normally:

بِسۡمِ ٱللَّهِ bis mil laa hi

بِـٱللَّهِ bil laa hi

قُلِ ٱللَّهُمَّ qu lil laa hum ma

Note that, in the Madīnah Muṣ-ḥaf, the second laam in the words ٱللَّهُ and ٱللَّهُمَّ only has a fat-ḥah but is pronounced as a long vowel ‘a’. There is nothing, however, in the writing of these words to show the lengthening of the vowel.

(Elsewhere, these words are usually written with a suspended alif:

ٱللّٰهُمَّ and ٱللّٰهُ .)

ٱللَّهُ   هُوَ ٱللَّهُ   إِنَّ ٱللَّهَ 1

لَآ إِلَـٰهَ إِلَّا ٱللَّهُ 2

كِتَـٰبُ ٱللَّهِ   رَسُولُ ٱللَّهِ 3

فَضْلُ ٱللَّهِ 4

لِلَّهِ   بِسْمِ ٱللَّهِ   ٱلْحَمْدُ لِلَّهِ 5

ءَامَنَّا بِـٱللَّهِ 6

قُلِ ٱللَّهُمَّ   قَالُواْ ٱللَّهُمَّ   ٱللَّهُمَّ رَبَّنَا 7

قَدَرُواْ ٱللَّهَ 8

قُلْ هُوَ ٱللَّهُ أَحَدٌ   ٱللَّهُ ٱلصَّمَدُ 9

Notes for Unit 36

More practice with the definite article

The text in lines 1 - 8 opposite is taken from Sūrah al-Fātiḥah and the last ten surahs of the Qur'ān.

In line 2, the ٱ in the definite article ٱلْ at the beginning of an utterance, is always pronounced as a vowel 'a'.

ٱلْحَمْدُ = *al-ḥamdu*

In line 3, the ٱ in ٱهْدِ is pronounced with a vowel 'i' because the first vowel after it is a kasrah.

In line 9, the ٱ in ٱقْرَأْ is pronounced with a vowel 'i' because the first vowel after it is a fat-ḥah.

Lines 1 & 2: The لَّ in the words لِلَّهِ and بِسْمِ ٱللَّهِ is pronounced normally, but lengthened.

Line 7. The لَّ in the words نَصْرُ ٱللَّهِ and ٱللَّهُ is pronounced 'lau', a rounded sound, but lengthened.

As an exercise, point out the words on the opposite page which are defined by the definite article. Write the words beginning with a 'moon' letter in one column and those beginning with a 'sun' letter in another.

A simple rule

When a letter with a vowel is followed by a letter with a sukūn or a shaddah - all the intervening letter(s) are ignored in pronunciation.

For example, in line 3 opposite,

ٱهْدِنَا ٱلصِّرَٰطَ = *ih di naṣ ṣi raa ṭa.*

The two alifs and the laam (all tinted) after the nūn are not pronounced.

The sentence, وَعَمِلُوا۟ ٱلصَّٰلِحَٰتِ is pronounced: *wa 'a mi luṣ ṣā li ḥā ti.*

For ease in pronunciation

All 'sun' letters are pronounced from points at the front of the mouth which are very close to where the letter 'laam' originates. This is why there is the process of merging in which the laam of the definite article is dropped in pronunciation and the following sun letter doubled. It all makes for greater ease in pronunciation.

1 بِسۡمِ ٱللَّهِ ٱلرَّحۡمَٰنِ ٱلرَّحِيمِ

2 ٱلۡحَمۡدُ لِلَّهِ رَبِّ ٱلۡعَٰلَمِينَ

3 ٱهۡدِنَا ٱلصِّرَٰطَ ٱلۡمُسۡتَقِيمَ

4 غَيۡرِ ٱلۡمَغۡضُوبِ عَلَيۡهِمۡ وَلَا ٱلضَّآلِّينَ

5 بِأَصۡحَٰبِ ٱلۡفِيلِ رِحۡلَةَ ٱلشِّتَآءِ وَٱلصَّيۡفِ

6 أَرَءَيۡتَ ٱلَّذِى يُكَذِّبُ بِٱلدِّينِ

7 إِذَا جَآءَ نَصۡرُ ٱللَّهِ وَٱلۡفَتۡحُ ٱللَّهُ ٱلصَّمَدُ

8 قُلۡ أَعُوذُ بِرَبِّ ٱلۡفَلَقِ مِنَ ٱلۡجِنَّةِ وَٱلنَّاسِ

9 ٱقۡرَأۡ بِٱسۡمِ رَبِّكَ ٱلَّذِى خَلَقَ

Notes for Unit 37

Special Signs & Fine Points

In the Madīnah Muṣ-ḥaf, the أْ , وْ , and ىْ with a small circle are always ignored in pronunciation.

ءَامَنُواْ aa ma nuu

أُوْلَـٰٓئِكَ u laa 'i ka

بِأَيْـيْدٍ bi ay di

مِاْئَةَ mi 'a ta

أُوْلُواْ ٱلْأَلْبَابِ u lul al baa bi

مَلَإِيْهِمْ ma la 'i him

A وٰ - wāw with a suspended alif directly above it is ignored in pronunciation:

رِبَوٰاْ ri baa صَلَوٰةٍ ṣa laa tin

A small oval shape is placed over a final alif in أَنَا and لَـٰكِنَّا .

This alif with the oval shape over it does not lengthen the vowel 'a' when no pause is made before the word following:

أَنَا بَشَرٌ ana ba sha run

لَـٰكِنَّا هُوَ ٱللَّهُ laa kinna hu wal lau hu

A small diamond shape is placed under the rau in مَجْرِىٰهَا to indicate that it should be read with a long vowel 'i' instead of the following long vowel 'a': *maj ree haa*

In the two words خَيْرًا ٱلْوَصِيَّةُ the tanwīn is followed by a hamzatu-l waṣl.

In such a case, there are two vowelless consonants coming together - the 'n' of the tanwīn and the laam with the sukūn. To correct this phonetic problem, a vowel 'i' is added after the 'n' of the tanwīn. The phrase is then read: *khay ra **ni** l wa ṣī ya tu.*

نُوحٌ ٱبْنَهُ is read *nū ḥu **ni** b na hu.*

In line 7, each word has a ط followed by a ت . In each case, the ṭau is sounded and then merged without a break to end with the taa'.

In line 8, a صـ with a small س above it is pronounced as a س .
However, a صـ with a small س below it is pronounced as a ص .

In line 9, the vowelless nūn in نُـجِى is pronounced as having a sukūn on it.

1 ءَامَنُوا۟ قُولُوا۟ يَرَوْا۟ خَلَوْا۟ مِا۟ئَةَ

2 نَبَإِى۟ بِأَيْي۟دٍ مَلَإِي۟هِمْ بِسْمِ ٱللَّهِ مَجْر۪ىٰهَا

3 أُو۟لُوا۟ ٱلْأَلْبَٰبِ أُو۟لِى أُو۟لَٰٓئِكَ

4 أَنَا۠ بَشَرٌ أَنَا۠ عَابِدٌ أَنَا۠ أُحْىِ

5 صَلَوٰةَ زَكَوٰةَ مِشْكَوٰةٍ رِبَوٰا۟ حَيَوٰةِ

6 قَوْمًا ٱللَّهُ خَيْرًا ٱلْوَصِيَّةُ نُوحٌ ٱبْنَهُۥ

7 بَسَطتَ أَحَطتَ فَرَّطتُمْ فَرَّطتَ

8 وَٱللَّهُ يَقْبِضُ وَيَبْصُۜطُ ٱلْمُصَۣيْطِرُونَ

9 وَكَذَٰلِكَ نُۨجِى ٱلْمُؤْمِنِينَ

SECTION SIX

Mi̱m & Nu̱n

Notes for Unit 38

Pronunciation of the م and ن

The ن with a suk<u>u</u>n - pronounced distinctly - *izh<u>a</u>r*

A 'nūn' which has a sukūn written on it is pronounced clearly and distinctly - with no lingering on it - when it is followed by one of the throat letters:

ء ح خ ع غ هـ

In each of the six examples below, the nūn with a sukūn is followed by one of the six letters above.

مِنْ أَيِّ min ay yi

مِنْ حَمِيمٍ min ḥa mī min

مَنْ خَلَقْتُ man kha laq tu

أَنْـعَمْتَ an 'am ta

أَنْ غَضِبَ an gha ḍi ba

تَـنْهَرْ tan har

Tanw<u>i</u>n - a vowelless n<u>u</u>n

The distinct pronunciation of the nūn also applies to tanwīn, because the *n* of the tanwīn is as a vowelless nūn. Do <u>not</u> linger on this tanwīn.

In this case the tanwīn is written: ً ٍ ٌ as in the words below:

سَوَآءٌ عَلَيْهِمْ sa waa 'un 'alay him

رَغَدًا حَيْثُ ra gha dan ḥay thu

شَيْءٍ عَلِيمٌ shay in 'a liim

This clear pronouncing is known as **iẓhār**. Iẓhār means 'making clear'.

The م with a suk<u>u</u>n

A 'mīm' with a sukūn is also pronounced clearly and distinctly - with no lingering on it - when the following letter is not م or ب.

لَهُمْ جَنَّـٰتٌ la hum jan naa tun

لَمْ يَلِدْ lam yalid.

(Note: When the following letter is a Mīm or Bā', the Mīm is written <u>without sukūn</u> and pronounced with ghunnah. For examples, see line 9 opposite.)

أ ء ح خ ع غ هـ 1

مِنْ أَيِّ مِنْ أَنفُسِهِمْ مِنْ حَمِيمٍ يَنْحِتُونَ 2

مِنْ خَوْفٍ أَنْعَمْتَ مِنْ عِلْمٍ 3

أَنْ غَضِبَ مِنْ غِلٍّ عَنْهُ تَنْهَرْ يَنْهَىٰ 4

عَذَابٌ أَلِيمٌ حَاسِدٍ إِذَا حَسَدَ طَيْرًا أَبَابِيلَ 5

نَارًا حَامِيَةً نَارًا خَالِدَةً شَيْءٍ عَلِيمٌ 6

قَوْمًا غَضِبَ فَرِيقًا هَدَى 7

أَلَمْ تَرَ لَمْ يَلِدْ هُمْ عَنْهَا لَهُمْ جَنَّٰتٌ 8

أَلَمْ يَعْلَم بِأَنَّ هُم بَعْدَ حَكَمْتُم بَيْنَ 9

Notes for Unit 39

Pronunciation of the م and ن

Complete merging - *idghām kāmil*

The letters in line 1 opposite are those involved in merging, explained below.

Nun without sukun

When a vowelless nūn is followed directly by one of the following letters

ل ر م ن

1 the vowelless nūn has no sukūn.
2 it is dropped in pronunciation.
3 a shaddah is placed on the laam, rau, meem or nūn.

This process is known as **idghām kāmil** - 'complete merging' or 'complete assimilation':

مَن لَّهُ mal lahu

مِن رَّبِّهِمۡ mir rab bi him

When the vowelless nūn is followed by laam or rau, there is no ghunnah.

Tanwin is a vowelless nūn; the above rules apply. It is then written staggered.

وَيۡلٌ لِّ waylul li

When the vowelless nūn is followed by a mīm or a nūn, a shaddah is placed on the following mīm or nūn and the humming or nasal sound is produced.

مِن نَّذِير minn na dhir

مِن مَّآءٍ mimm maaaa 'in

Tanwin is a vowelless nūn; the above rules apply. It is then written staggered

بِحِجَارَةٍ مِّن bi ḥijaara timm min

In fact, wherever a mīm or nūn occurs with a shaddah, it should always be pronounced with ghunnah - the humming nasal sound - equal to two

لَمَّا lamm maa

مِنَ ٱلۡجِنَّةِ وَ النَّاسِ mina-l jinn nati wa-nn naas

Mim without sukun

A final vowelless mīm is written without sukūn when it is followed by a word beginning with another mīm. This latter mīm will have a shaddah and is pronounded with ghunnah.

هُم مِّنۡهَا humm min haa

أَم مَّنۡ amm man

Sequence of identical letters

When two identical letters follow each other in the same word (or at the end of one word and the beginning of another) and the first such letter has no vowel or sign while the following letter has a shaddah, the bare letter is dropped in pronunciation:

يُدۡرِككُّم yud rik kum

قَد دَّخَلَ qad da kha la

ى ر م ل و ن يَرْمِلُونَ 1

مِن رَّبِّهِمْ أَن رَّءَاهُ مِن رِّجَالِكُمْ 2

وَلَمْ يَكُن لَّهُ مَن لَّهُ مِن لَّدُنكَ 3

مِن مَّآءٍ مِن مَّلَكٍ حَبْلٌ مِّن مَّسَدٍ 4

إِن نَّحْنُ مِن نَّذِيرٍ مِن نِّسَآئِكُمْ 5

غَفُورًا رَّحِيمًا غَفُورٌ رَّحِيمٌ غَفُورٍ رَّحِيمٍ 6

وَيْلٌ لِّكُلِّ هُمَزَةٍ لُّمَزَةٍ مَتَاعًا لَّكُمْ 7

بِحِجَارَةٍ مِّن سِجِّيلٍ كَعَصْفٍ مَّأْكُولٍ 8

هُم مِّنْهَا أَم مَّن فِى قُلُوبِهِم مَّرَضٌ 9

Notes for Unit 40

Complete merging - *idghām kāmil*

Assimilation in sequence of similar letters

Some letters are dropped completely in pronunciation when followed by a similar sounding letter. The dropped letter is written completely bare, without sukūn or vowel.

When followed by a taa', a daal is dropped in pronunciation:

قَد تَّبَيَّنَ qat tabayyana

مَهَدتُّ mahat tu

When followed by a daal, a taa is dropped in pronunciation:

أُجِيبَت دَّعْوَتُكُمَا ujiibad da'watukumaa

When followed by a ṭau, a taa' is dropped in pronunciation:

وَدَّت طَّآئِفَةٌ waddaṭ ṭā'ifatun

When followed by a ẓau, the dhaal is not pronounced:

إِذ ظَّلَمْتُمْ iẓ ẓalamtum

When followed by a mīm, a baa' is not pronounced:

وَ ٱرْكَب مَّعَنَا wa-r kam ma'a naa

When followed by a rau, a laam is not pronounced:

قُل رَّبِّ qur rabbi

When followed by a dhaal, a thaa is not pronounced:

يَلْهَث ذَّٰلِكَ yal hadh dhaalika

When followed by a kaaf, the qaaf is not pronounced:

نَخْلُقكُّمْ nakhluk kum

The ط followed by a ت

In the following words, begin pronouncing a ط (without articulating it fully) and then move seamlessly to finish with an audible ت .

فَرَّطتُمْ فَرَّطتَ أَحَطتَ بَسَطتَ

عَبَدتُّمْ قَد تَّبَيَّنَ مَهَدتُّ 1

أُجِيبَت دَّعْوَتُكُمَا 2

قَالَت طَّآئِفَةٌ وَدَّت طَّآئِفَةٌ 3

إِذ ظَّلَمْتُمْ 4

ٱرْكَب مَّعَنَا 5

يَلْهَث ذَّٰلِكَ 6

نَخْلُقكُّمْ 7

قُل رَّبِّ زِدْنِى عِلْمًا بَل رَّفَعَهُ ٱللَّهُ 8

فَرَّطتُمْ فَرَّطتَ أَحَطتَ بَسَطتَ 9

Notes for Unit 41

Pronunciation of the م and ن

Incomplete merging - *idghām nāqis*

Incomplete merging occurs when the vowelless nūn is followed by a wāw or a yā'.

It is called incomplete because
1 the nūn is not completely lost
2 the wāw or yā' is not completely doubled.

In this case, therefore, the wāw or yā' does not have the shaddah (as is the case with lām and rā' where complete merging takes place).

Ghunnah is observed with all incomplete merging.

In all cases of merging, the vowelless nūn remains completely bare - it carries no sukūn sign. See lines 1 and 2.

Staggered tanwin

Incomplete merging - with ghunnah - also applies after tanwīn followed by a wāw or a yā'.

In this case the tanwīn will be written staggered: ـࣰ ـࣲ ـࣱ.

This shows that ghunnah should be observed. See lines 3 - 6 opposite.

Conversion (إِقۡلَاب)

When the vowelless nūn is immediately followed by a bā', it is converted into a mīm sound.

To indicate this, a small mīm is then written over the nūn.

This mīm is lengthened to about two ḥarakahs and pronounced with the pleasant humming sound or ghunnah.

This process is called iqlāb or conversion (of the mīm to a nūn).

جَنۢبِ jamm bi

مِنۢ بَعۡدِ mimm ba'di

بِذَنۢبِهِمۡ bidhamm bihim

Iqlab also applies to tanwin followed by a ba'.

In this case the tanwīn will be written as follows: ـَۢ ـِۭ ـُۢ.

عَوَانُۢ بَيۡنَ 'awaanumm bayna

سَمِيعًۢا بَصِيرًا samii'amm baṣiiran

كِرَامِۭ بَرَرَةٍ kiraamimm bararatin

For more examples, see lines 7 and 8.

- Observe how tanwīn is written in the three words in line 9 opposite.

1 مِن وَلِيٍّ مِن وَرَآءِ إِن وَهَبَ

2 مَن يَعْمَلْ مَن يَخْشَى أَن يَضْرِبَ

3 مَالًا وَ عَدَّدَهُ

4 غِشَاوَةٌ وَلَهُمْ مِسْكِينًا وَ يَتِيمًا

5 يَومَئِذٍ وَاجِفَةٌ لَهَبٍ وَ تَبَّ

6 كِتَـٰبًا يَسِيرًا خَيْرًا يَرَهُۥ شَرًّا يَرَهُۥ

7 مِنۢ بَعْدِ مِنۢ بَيْنِ جَنۢبِ بِذَنۢبِهِمْ

8 سَمِيعًۢا بَصِيرًا كِرَامٍۢ بَرَرَةٍ

9 صُمٌّۢ بُكْمٌ عُمْىٌ

Notes for Unit 42

Pronunciation of the م and ن

The ن with no sukun - pronounced indistinctly - *ikhfa'*

A bare vowelless nūn is sometimes pronounced indistinctly with some *ghunnah* and lengthened.
This indistinct pronunciation is known as ikhfā' - إخفاء - which literally means 'concealing' or 'lowering of the voice'.

The vowelless nūn is pronounced indistinctly when:

1 The nūn has no sukūn
2 There is no shaddah over the letter that follows the nūn
3 The letter after the nūn is not:
   a. one of the throat letters involved in iẓhār: ء ح خ ع غ هـ
   b. one of the merging (idghām) letters: ل ر م ن
   c. a bā' (requiring conversion or iqlāb of the nūn into a mīm)

In pronouncing the nūn indistinctly, linger on it for about two lengths or *ḥarakahs* and produce some *ghunnah* or humming.
Ikhfā' applies to the vowelless nūn in the words in lines 1- 4 opposite.

• Note the letter which comes immediately after the vowelless nūn.

Staggered tanwin
The *n* of the tanwīn is a vowelless nūn and so the above rules (2) and (3) of ikhfā' apply. Note the letter immediately after the tanwīn.
To make it easy for the reader, the tanwīn in these cases is written in a staggered fashion.
See lines 5 - 9 opposite.

The م with no sukun

A final vowelless mīm is written without sukūn when it is followed by a word beginning with a bā'. This mīm is pronounced indistinctly - the lips do not make full contact when it is proounced. (See Unit 38, line 9.)

يَعْلَم بِأَنَّ ya'lamm bi'anna

هُم بَعْدَ humm ba'da.

1 أَنتَ أَنتُمۡ أُنثَىٰ مَن جَآءَ أَندَادًا مُنذُ

2 أَنزَلَ ٱلۡإِنسَانُ فَمَن شَهِدَ وَلِـمَن صَبَرَ

3 مَن ضَلَّ مِن طَيِّبَٰتِ مِن ظُهُورِهَا

4 فَإِن فَآءُو مَن كَانَ مِنكُمۡ

5 جَنَّٰتٍ تَجۡرِي خَيۡرٌ ثَوَابًا فَصَبۡرٌ جَمِيلٌ

6 كَأۡسًا دِهَاقًا عَزِيزٌ ذُو نَفۡسًا زَكِيَّةً

7 قَوۡلًا سَدِيدًا لِنَفۡسٍ شَيۡـًٔا نَخِيلٌ صِنوَانٌ

8 قُوَّةٍ ضَعۡفًا حَلَٰلًا طَيِّبًا ظِلًّا ظَلِيلًا

9 مَرَضٌ فَزَادَ عَذَابٌ قَرِيبٌ عُلُوًّا كَبِيرًا

SECTION SEVEN

Pausing & Supplications

Notes for Unit 43

Pausing

In reciting the Qur'ān, there are rules to be observed when stopping at the end of a verse, or in the middle of a verse to take breath.

The following should be observed if you stop or pause at:

1 A word ending in fat-ḥah tanwīn and an alif. The 'n' of the tanwīn is not pronounced, but the alif lengthens the vowel 'a':

أَفْوَاجًا pronounced أَفْوَاجَا - *af waa jaa.*

2 A word ending in fat-ḥah tanwīn and an alif maqṣūrah. The 'n' of the tanwīn is not pronounced and the alif maqṣūrah lengthens the vowel 'a':

طُوًى pronounced طُوَا - *ṭu waa.*

3 A word ending with a fat-ḥah tanwīn on a hamzah. The 'n' of the tanwīn is not pronounced and the fat-ḥah is pronounced as a long vowel 'a':

نِسَآءً pronounced نِسَآءَا - *nisaaaa 'aa.*

4 A word ending in tā' marbūṭah. The tā' marbūṭah is pronounced as a vowelless haa':

بَقَرَةٌ pronounced بَقَرَهْ - *baqarah.*

5 A word ending with a haa' and followed by a small wāw or yā': the wāw or yā' is made silent while the hā' is made vowelless:

لَهُۥ pronounced لَهْ - *lah.*

بِهِۦ pronounced بِهْ - *bih.*

1 إِنَّهُۥ كَانَ تَوَّابًا   فِى دِينِ ٱللَّهِ أَفْوَاجًا

2 بِٱلْوَادِ ٱلْمُقَدَّسِ طُوًى   يَتْبَعُهَآ أَذًى

3 رِجَالًا كَثِيرًا وَنِسَآءً   لَيْسُواْ سَوَآءً

4 تَصْلَىٰ نَارًا حَامِيَةً   مِنْهُمْ تُقَىٰةً

5 أَبْصَٰرُهَا خَٰشِعَةٌ

6 كِرَامٍۭ بَرَرَةٍ

7 مِنْ أَىِّ شَىْءٍ خَلَقَهُۥ   وَلَوْ أَلْقَىٰ مَعَاذِيرَهُۥ

8 لِتَعْجَلَ بِهِۦٓ

9 فَلْيَنظُرِ ٱلْإِنسَٰنُ إِلَىٰ طَعَامِهِۦٓ

Notes for Unit 44

Pausing (*continued*)

The following should be observed when pausing at words ending in alif, wāw or yā':

1 If the wāw, yā' or alif is bare or has a fat-ḥah, it is pronounced as a long vowel, e.g.

هُوَ is pronounced هُو (*hoo*);

هِيَ is pronounced هِي (*hee*);

لَهَا is pronounced لَهَا; (*la haa*);

قَالُوْا is pronounced قَالُوْا; (*qaa loo*);

A bare yā' preceded by a fat-ḥah is an alif maqṣūrah, and is pronounced as a long vowel 'a': عِيسَى *'ee saa;* هُدَى *hu daa*

2 If the wāw or yā' has a shaddah, it is doubled and the accompanying short vowel or tanwīn sign is ignored:

عَدُوٌّ pronounced *'a duww;*

إِلَيَّ pronounced *i layy*

3 If the final letter is a yā', or analif with an oval shape, it is pronounced as a long vowel: أَنَا *a naa;* يَخْشَىٰ *yakh shaa*

In other circumstances, the final letter is made vowelless when pausing: قُرَيْشٍ pronounced *qu raysh*

When a pause is made on a word ending with one of the qalqalah letters (قطب جد), qalqalah must be made:

فَلَقِ pronounced *fa laqq;*

أَحَدٌ pronounced *a ḥadd.*

1 لَآ إِلَـٰهَ إِلَّا هُوَ

2 يُبَيِّن لَّنَا مَا هِىَ

3 بِأَنَّ رَبَّكَ أَوْحَىٰ لَهَا   مَن دَسَّىٰهَا

4 وَٱدْخُلِى جَنَّتِى

5 سَبِّحِ ٱسْمَ رَبِّكَ ٱلْأَعْلَى   ٱلَّذِى خَلَقَ فَسَوَّى

6 بَعْضُكُمْ لِبَعْضٍ عَدُوٌّ

7 فَٱللَّهُ هُوَ ٱلْوَلِىُّ

8 مِمَّ خُلِقَ   وَإِخْوَانُ لُوطٍ   إِذَا وَقَبَ

9 كُلِّ زَوْجٍۭ بَهِيجٍ   لَمْ يَلِدْ وَلَمْ يُولَدْ

Notes for Unit 45

Stopping or Pausing Signs

In reciting the Qur'ān, stopping or pausing is done
1 at the end of a verse;
2 within a verse, as indicated by certain letters and signs;
3 for regaining breath.

Stopping or Pausing Signs:

م Must stop otherwise the meaning may be altered or distorted.

لا No stop. لا means 'No'. The reciter has to continue reading without any pause.

ج Permissible to stop, but no preference implied for either stopping or continuing.
ج is short for جائز, meaning 'allowed'.

صلے Permissible to stop, but preferable to continue.

قلے Preferable to stop, but permitted to continue.

∴ ∴ (Called mu'aanaqah or 'embracing'). Three dots, placed over successive words, indicate an option to pause at one or the other, but not at both.

س A small 'seen' indicating a pause is required at the letter over which it occurs, without taking a breath.

(This has nothing to do with a small 'seen' placed either above or below a ṣaad.
This 'seen' is pronounced as a 'seen' when it is above the ṣaad;
It is pronounced as a ṣaad when the 'seen' is below the ṣaad.)

1 أَأَنتُمْ أَشَدُّ خَلْقًا أَمِ ٱلسَّمَآءُ ۚ بَنَىٰهَا

2 كَلَّا ۖ بَل لَّا تُكْرِمُونَ ٱلْيَتِيمَ

3 تِلْكَ أَمَانِيُّهُمْ ۗ هَاتُوا۟ بُرْهَانَكُمْ

4 وَأُخْرَىٰ تُحِبُّونَهَا ۖ نَصْرٌ مِّنَ ٱللَّهِ وَفَتْحٌ

5 قَرِيبٌ ۗ وَبَشِّرِ ٱلْمُؤْمِنِينَ

6 مَاذَآ أَرَادَ ٱللَّهُ بِهَٰذَا مَثَلًا ۘ يُضِلُّ بِهِۦ كَثِيرًا

7 كَلَّا ۖ بَلْ ۜ رَانَ عَلَىٰ قُلُوبِهِم

8 ذَٰلِكَ ٱلْكِتَٰبُ لَا رَيْبَ ۛ فِيهِ ۛ هُدًى لِّلْمُتَّقِينَ

9 وَلِلَّهِ ٱلْمَشْرِقُ وَٱلْمَغْرِبُ ۚ فَأَيْنَمَا تُوَلُّوا۟

Notes for Unit 46

Sujud at-Tilawah

While reciting the Qur'ān, there are fourteen places where a *sajdah* or prostration should be performed. (*Sujūd* means prostration; *sajdah* means an act of prostration; *tilāwah* means reciting.)

In the Qur'ānic text, a horizontal line is placed over the word(s) which give the reason for prostration. كَلَّا لَا تُطِعْهُ وَاسْجُدْ وَاقْتَرِب ۩

A prostration sign within the text ۩ then indicates the exact point at which the prostration is to be performed.

A sign with the word (سجدة) is placed in the margin.

سَجْدَة

To perform the sajdah, face the qiblah and prostrate just once as in Ṣalāh. While prostrating, you may make a supplication (du'ā').

During Salah

While performing Ṣalāh, you must perform a sajdah at any point in the recitation where it is required.
From your standing position, go directly to the prostrating position.
After the prostration, stand up and continue reciting some more verses of the Qur'ān, and then continue with the rest of the Ṣalāh.

The meaning of the verses with the sajdah opposite is:
Say: Whether you believe in it (the Qur'ān) or not, it is true that those who were given knowledge beforehand, when it is recited to them, fall down on their faces in humble prostration.
And they say: Glory to our Sustainer! Truly has the promise of our Sustainer been fulfilled.
They fall down on their faces in tears, and it increases them in humility.
(*Sūrah al-Isrā'*, 17: 107-109).

قُلْ ءَامِنُوا۟ بِهِۦٓ أَوْ لَا تُؤْمِنُوٓا۟ ۚ إِنَّ ٱلَّذِينَ أُوتُوا۟ ٱلْعِلْمَ مِن قَبْلِهِۦٓ إِذَا يُتْلَىٰ
عَلَيْهِمْ يَخِرُّونَ لِلْأَذْقَانِ سُجَّدًا ﴿١٠٧﴾ وَيَقُولُونَ سُبْحَٰنَ رَبِّنَآ إِن كَانَ
وَعْدُ رَبِّنَا لَمَفْعُولًا ﴿١٠٨﴾ وَيَخِرُّونَ لِلْأَذْقَانِ يَبْكُونَ وَيَزِيدُهُمْ
خُشُوعًا ۩ ﴿١٠٩﴾ سجدة

Notes for Unit 47

Requirements

While reciting the Qur'ān, you should be clean and in a state of wuḍū'. You should recite with the aim of seeking Allah's pleasure and favour.

At the start of Qur'ān reading, whether at the beginning of a sūrah or at any point, you should seek Allāh's protection (see sūrah an-Naḥl, 16: 98) by saying:

أَعُوذُ بِـٱللَّهِ مِنَ ٱلشَّيْطَانِ ٱلرَّجِيمِ

I seek Allāh's protection from Satan, the rejected.

And at the beginning of every sūrah, except Sūrah at-Tawbah (s.9), you should say:

بِسۡمِ ٱللَّهِ ٱلرَّحۡمَٰنِ ٱلرَّحِيمِ

In the name of Allāh, the Most Gracious, the Ever Merciful.

Supplications

Supplications express the human need, always, for Divine guidance and support. The Qur'ān and the sayings of the Prophet, peace be on him, abound in du'ās or supplications that are the most appropriate for our human needs and aspirations.

The supplication or du'ā' in lines 3-5 opposite is based on verses from sūrah al-Ḥujurāt (s.49, v.7).

The supplication or du'ā' in lines 6-7 opposite is from sūrah al-Baqarah (2: 201).

The meaning of the text:

1 I seek Allāh's protection from satan, the rejected.
2 In the name of Allāh, the Most Gracious, the Ever Merciful.
3 O Allāh, Our Sustainer! Make true faith (in You) dear to us and adorn it in our hearts, (4) and make hateful to us all rejection of and ingratitude to You, and all wickedness and disobedience, (5) and make us among the rightly-guided.
6 Our Sustainer! Give us good in this world,
7 And good in the hereafter and save us from the punishment of the fire,
8 And cause us to enter Paradise with the virtuous,
9 O Almighty, Forgiving, Sustainer of all the worlds.

1 أَعُوذُ بِـٱللَّهِ مِنَ ٱلشَّيْطَانِ ٱلرَّجِيمِ

2 بِسْمِ ٱللَّهِ ٱلرَّحْمَٰنِ ٱلرَّحِيمِ

3 ٱللَّهُمَّ رَبَّنَا حَبِّبْ إِلَيْنَا ٱلْإِيمَانَ وَزَيِّنْهُ فِى قُلُوبِنَا

4 وَ كَرِّهْ إِلَيْنَا ٱلْكُفْرَ وَٱلْفُسُوقَ وَٱلْعِصْيَانَ

5 وَٱجْعَلْنَا مِنَ ٱلرَّاشِدِينَ

6 رَبَّنَآ ءَاتِنَا فِى ٱلدُّنيَا حَسَنَةً

7 وَ فِى ٱلْأَخِرَةِ حَسَنَةً وَ قِنَا عَذَابَ ٱلنَّارِ

8 وَ أَدْخِلْنَا ٱلْجَنَّةَ مَعَ ٱلْأَبْرَارِ

9 يَا عَزِيزُ يَا غَفَّارُ يَا رَبَّ ٱلْعَـٰلَمِينَ

Notes for Unit 48

Benefits and rewards

Several ḥadīths or sayings of the Prophet Muhammad, may Allāh bless him and grant him peace, stress the importance of the regular and proficient reading of the Qur'ān:

'Read the Qur'ān for it comes as an advocate for its readers on the day of Judgement.' *(Muslim)*

'The best among you are those who learn the Qur'ān and teach it.' *(Bukhārī)*

'The one who reads the Qur'ān and is proficient in it will, on the day of Judgement, be among the most noble and virtuous, and the one who recites the Qur'ān with difficulty, stumbling over its words, shall have a double reward.' *(Bukhārī and Muslim)*

Supplications on the Qur'an

The meaning of the du'ās on the opposite page is:

O Allāh, make the Qur'ān the sweet spring of (freshness and joy in) our hearts, the light of our breasts, and the removal of our woes.

O Allah, grant me grace through the Glorious Qur'ān,
and make it for me a leader, a light, a source of guidance and mercy.

O Allah, cause me to remember what I have forgotten of it, and teach me of it what I do not know.

Enable me to recite it during the night and during the day,
And make it a testimony on my behalf (on the day of Judgement),
O Sustainer of all the worlds!

And our final supplication is: All praise and gratitude is to Allāh,
the Sustainer of all the worlds!

1 ٱللَّهُمَّ ٱجْعَلِ ٱلْقُرْءَانَ رَبِيعَ قُلُوبِنَا

2 وَ نُورَ صُدُورِنَا وَ جَلَآءَ أَحْزَانِنَا

3 ٱللَّهُمَّ ٱرْحَمْنِى بِـٱلْقُرْءَانِ ٱلْعَظِيمِ

4 وَٱجْعَلْهُ لِىَ إِمَامًا وَنُورًا وَ هُدًى وَرَحْمَةً

5 ٱللَّهُمَّ ذَكِّرْنِى مِنْهُ مَا نَسِيتُ

6 وَ عَلِّمْنِى مِنْهُ مَا جَهِلْتُ

7 وَٱرْزُقْنِى تِلَاوَتَهُۥ أَنَآءَ ٱلَّيْلِ وَ أَنَآءَ ٱلنَّهَارِ

8 وَٱجْعَلْهُ لِى حُجَّةً يَا رَبَّ ٱلْعَٰلَمِينَ

9 وَءَاخِرُ دَعْوَٰنَا أَنِ ٱلْحَمْدُ لِلَّهِ رَبِّ ٱلْعَٰلَمِينَ

SECTION EIGHT

Short Surahs

S<u>u</u>rah al-Faatihah

The Opening

1 In the name of *Allāh*, the Most Gracious, the Ever Merciful
2 All praise and gratitude is due to Allah,
The Sustainer of all the worlds.
3 The Most Gracious, the Ever Merciful.
4 Ruler of the Day of Judgement.
5 You do we worship and You do we ask for help.
6 Guide us the straight way,
7 The way of those whom You have blessed,
Not of those who deserve Your anger,
Nor of those who are astray.

- The above numbers refer to verse numbers.

Test your knowledge of the script

1. How should you pronounce the first alif with the hamzatu-waṣl in lines 3 and 4 - as with a fat-ḥah, a kasrah or a ḍammah?
2. How should you pronounce the first alif with the hamzatu-wasl in line 7 - as with a fat-ḥah, a kasrah or a ḍammah?
3. A nūn is sometimes written without a sukūn. Why is there a sukūn on the nūn in أنعمت (line 8)? How is this nūn pronounced:
   a. with ghunnah and lengthened, or
   b. distinctly, and short without lingering?
4. What effect does the shaddah on the laam in ضالين have on the pronunciation of the preceding maddah (line 9)?

For answers to:

question 1, see Unit 33, Rule 1; question 2, see Unit 33, Rule 2; question 3, see Unit 38; question 4, see Unit 32.

سُورَةُ الفَاتِحَة 1

بِسْمِ ٱللَّهِ ٱلرَّحْمَٰنِ ٱلرَّحِيمِ ﴿١﴾ 2

ٱلْحَمْدُ لِلَّهِ رَبِّ ٱلْعَٰلَمِينَ ﴿٢﴾ 3

ٱلرَّحْمَٰنِ ٱلرَّحِيمِ ﴿٣﴾ 4

مَٰلِكِ يَوْمِ ٱلدِّينِ ﴿٤﴾ 5

إِيَّاكَ نَعْبُدُ وَإِيَّاكَ نَسْتَعِينُ ﴿٥﴾ 6

ٱهْدِنَا ٱلصِّرَٰطَ ٱلْمُسْتَقِيمَ ﴿٦﴾ 7

صِرَٰطَ ٱلَّذِينَ أَنْعَمْتَ عَلَيْهِمْ 8

غَيْرِ ٱلْمَغْضُوبِ عَلَيْهِمْ وَلَا ٱلضَّآلِّينَ ﴿٧﴾ 9

S<u>u</u>rah al-'Asr

Time

In the name of Allāh, the Most Gracious, the Ever Merciful

1 By Time!
2 Surely the human being is in loss
3 Except those who have true faith,
do righteous deeds,
and encourage one another in (upholding the) truth,
and encourage one another in steadfastness.

Test your knowledge of the script

1. How should you pronounce the nūn with the shaddah in إنّ (line 4)?
2. Why is there no sukūn on the first nūn in إنسن (line 8)? How is this nūn pronounced:
   a. indistinctly with ghunnah and lengthened, or
   b. distinctly without lingering?
3. In line 6, what happens in pronunciation to the four letters after the first laam?

For answers to:

question 1, see Unit 21; question 2, see Unit 42;
question 3, see Unit 36.

سُورَةُ الْعَصْرِ

بِسْمِ ٱللَّهِ ٱلرَّحْمَٰنِ ٱلرَّحِيمِ

وَٱلْعَصْرِ ﴿١﴾

إِنَّ ٱلْإِنسَٰنَ لَفِى خُسْرٍ ﴿٢﴾

إِلَّا ٱلَّذِينَ ءَامَنُوا۟

وَعَمِلُوا۟ ٱلصَّٰلِحَٰتِ

وَتَوَاصَوْا۟ بِٱلْحَقِّ

وَتَوَاصَوْا۟ بِٱلصَّبْرِ ﴿٣﴾

Su̲rah al-Humazah

The Slanderer

In the name of Allāh, the Most Gracious, the Ever Merciful
1 Woe to every slanderer and backbiter
2 Who has gathered riches and counts them over,
3 Thinking that his riches will make him last forever.
4 By no means! He will be thrust into the Crusher.
5 And what will make you realise what the Crusher is?
6 (It is) the fire of God, kindled,
7 Rising over hearts,
8 Engulfing them
9 In columns leaping up.

Test your knowledge of the script

1. In line 3, point out the two examples of 'complete assimilation' *(idghām kāmil)*. How does assimilation affect the way in which tanwīn is written? (See Unit 39.)
2. In line 3, point out the one example of 'incomplete assimilation' *(idghām nāqiṣ)*. How does assimilation affect the way in which tanwīn is written? (See Unit 41.)
3. In line 4, why is there a maddah on the small wāw after ماله? (See Unit 26.)
4. In line 4, why is there a small mīm above the nūn in لينبذن? What is the changing of a nūn to a mīm called in Arabic? (See Unit 41.)
5. In line 5, what is the letter between rā' and kāf in أدرك called ? (See Unit 24.)
6. In line 6, what is the last letter in على called ? (See Unit 24.)
7. All the verses in this sūrah end with a *tā' marbūṭah* or a *hā'*. How should you pronounce these letters when pausing at the end of each verse? (See Unit 43.)
8. How do you pronounce the first alif with hamzatu-waṣl in line 6? (See U. 33.)
9. In pronunciation, what happens to the mīm in عليهم (line 7)? (See Unit 39.)
10. In pronunciaiton, what is the effect of the hamzah and the sukūn on the wāw in مؤصدة (line 8)? (See Unit 20.)
11. Point out an example of assimilation (*idghām*) with *ghunnah*. (See Unit 39.)

سُورَةُ ٱلْهُمَزَةِ

بِسْمِ ٱللَّهِ ٱلرَّحْمَٰنِ ٱلرَّحِيمِ

وَيْلٌ لِّكُلِّ هُمَزَةٍ لُّمَزَةٍ ﴿١﴾ ٱلَّذِى جَمَعَ مَالًا وَعَدَّدَهُۥ ﴿٢﴾

يَحْسَبُ أَنَّ مَالَهُۥٓ أَخْلَدَهُۥ ﴿٣﴾ كَلَّا ۖ لَيُنۢبَذَنَّ فِى ٱلْحُطَمَةِ ﴿٤﴾

وَمَآ أَدْرَىٰكَ مَا ٱلْحُطَمَةُ ﴿٥﴾ نَارُ ٱللَّهِ ٱلْمُوقَدَةُ ﴿٦﴾

ٱلَّتِى تَطَّلِعُ عَلَى ٱلْأَفْـِٔدَةِ ﴿٧﴾

إِنَّهَا عَلَيْهِم مُّؤْصَدَةٌ ﴿٨﴾

فِى عَمَدٍ مُّمَدَّدَةٍۭ ﴿٩﴾

Surah al-Fiil

The Elephant

In the name of Allāh, the Most Gracious, the Ever Merciful

1 Have you not seen how your Sustainer dealt with the owners (army) of the Elephant?
2 Did He not make their plan go astray?
3 And He sent against them swarms of flying creatures,
4 Pelting them with stones of Sijjīl.
5 So did He make them like a field of grain eaten (down to stubble).

Test your knowledge of the script

1. In line 5, why is the tanwīn in طيرا written as it is? How is this tanwīn pronounced:
   a. with ghunnah, or
   b. distinctly without lingering?
2. The last mīm in ترميهم has no sukūn. Why? What is the effect of this on the pronunciation of the mīm?
3. Point out two examples of assimilation (*idghām*) with *ghunnah.*
4. The nūn in من (line 6) has no sukūn. Why? What is the effect of this on the pronunciation of the nūn?
5. In pronunciation, what is the effect of the hamzah and the sukūn on the alif in مأكول (line 7)?

For answers to:

question 1, see Unit 14; question 2, see Unit 42;
question 3, see Unit 36; question 4, see Unit 42;
question 5, see Unit 39.

سُورَةُ ٱلْفِيلِ

بِسْمِ ٱللَّهِ ٱلرَّحْمَٰنِ ٱلرَّحِيمِ

أَلَمْ تَرَ كَيْفَ فَعَلَ رَبُّكَ بِأَصْحَٰبِ ٱلْفِيلِ ﴿١﴾

أَلَمْ يَجْعَلْ كَيْدَهُمْ فِى تَضْلِيلٍ ﴿٢﴾

وَأَرْسَلَ عَلَيْهِمْ طَيْرًا أَبَابِيلَ ﴿٣﴾

تَرْمِيهِم بِحِجَارَةٍ مِّن سِجِّيلٍ ﴿٤﴾

فَجَعَلَهُمْ كَعَصْفٍ مَّأْكُولٍ ﴿٥﴾

Su̲rah Quraysh

Quraysh

In the name of Allāh, the Most Gracious, the Ever Merciful

1 For the security of the Quraysh,
2 For their security during the journey of winter and of summer -
3 Let them, therefore, worship the Sustainer of this House,
4 He Who has given them food against hunger,
5 And made them safe from fear (of danger).

Test your knowledge of the script

1. Note the two ways in which the yā' is written in the first word of lines 3 and 4. What effect does each of these yā' have in pronunciation?
2. Why is there a maddah on the alif in شتاء (line 4)?
3. Why is there a maddah on the yā' in الذى (line 6)?
4. Why is there no sukūn on the nūn in من (line 6) but a sukūn on the nūn in من (line 7)? How is this nūn pronounced in either case:
   a. with ghunnah and lengthened, or
   b. distinctly, short without lingering?

For answers to:

question 1, see Unit 25; question 2, see Unit 31;
question 3, see Unit 31; question 4, see Units 42 and 38.

سُورَةُ قُرَيْشٍ

بِسْمِ ٱللَّهِ ٱلرَّحْمَٰنِ ٱلرَّحِيمِ

لِإِيلَٰفِ قُرَيْشٍ ﴿١﴾

إِۦلَٰفِهِمْ رِحْلَةَ ٱلشِّتَآءِ وَٱلصَّيْفِ ﴿٢﴾

فَلْيَعْبُدُوا۟ رَبَّ هَٰذَا ٱلْبَيْتِ ﴿٣﴾

ٱلَّذِىٓ أَطْعَمَهُم مِّن جُوعٍ

وَءَامَنَهُم مِّنْ خَوْفٍۭ ﴿٤﴾

Su<u>r</u>ah al-Maa'uun

Assistance

In the name of Allāh, the Most Gracious, the Ever Merciful

1 Have your observed the one who denies
the Dīn (true religion, the Judgement to come)?
2 That is the one who drives away the orphan,
3 And feels no urge to feed the poor.
4 Woe, then, unto those who pray
5 But are heedless of their Prayer;
6 Who (only) want to be seen (and praised)
7 But deny all assistance (to others).

Test your knowledge of the script

1. Point out one example of complete assimilation *(idghām kāmil).*
2. Why is there a maddah on the alif in يراءون (line 8)?
3. Why is there no sukūn on the nūn in عن (line 7)? How is this nūn pronounced:
   a. indistinctly with ghunnah, or
   b. distinctly without lingering?

For answers to:

question 1, see Unit 39; question 2, see Unit 31;
question 3, see Unit 42.

سُورَةُ المَاعُونِ 1

بِسْمِ ٱللَّهِ ٱلرَّحْمَٰنِ ٱلرَّحِيمِ 2

أَرَءَيْتَ ٱلَّذِى يُكَذِّبُ بِٱلدِّينِ ﴿١﴾ 3

فَذَٰلِكَ ٱلَّذِى يَدُعُّ ٱلْيَتِيمَ ﴿٢﴾ 4

وَلَا يَحُضُّ عَلَىٰ طَعَامِ ٱلْمِسْكِينِ ﴿٣﴾ 5

فَوَيْلٌ لِّلْمُصَلِّينَ ﴿٤﴾ 6

ٱلَّذِينَ هُمْ عَن صَلَاتِهِمْ سَاهُونَ ﴿٥﴾ 7

ٱلَّذِينَ هُمْ يُرَآءُونَ ﴿٦﴾ 8

وَيَمْنَعُونَ ٱلْمَاعُونَ ﴿٧﴾ 9

S<u>u</u>rah al-Kawthar

Abundance

In the name of Allāh, the Most Gracious, the Ever Merciful

1 Indeed We, We have given you (O Prophet) good in abundance;

2 So, pray to your Sustainer, and sacrifice.

3 Indeed, the one who hates you - he is the one cut off (from all that is good).

Test your knowledge of the script

1 Why is there a maddah on the alif in إنّا (line 3)?

2 What effect does a shaddah have on a nūn as in إنّ (line 5) and إنّا (line 3)?

3 What is the difference in meaning between إنّ (line 5) and إنّا (line 3)?

4 How is the nūn in وأنحر pronounced:
a. with ghunnah, or
b. distinctly and without lingering?

For answers to:

question 1, see Unit 31; question 2, see Unit 21;
question 3, see Unit 27; question 4, see Unit 38.

سُورَةُ الكَوْثَرِ

بِسْمِ اللَّهِ الرَّحْمَٰنِ الرَّحِيمِ

إِنَّآ أَعْطَيْنَٰكَ ٱلْكَوْثَرَ ﴿١﴾

فَصَلِّ لِرَبِّكَ وَٱنْحَرْ ﴿٢﴾

إِنَّ شَانِئَكَ هُوَ ٱلْأَبْتَرُ ﴿٣﴾

S<u>u</u>rah al-Kaafiruun

Those who deny the Truth

In the name of Allāh, the Most Gracious, the Ever Merciful

1 Say: O you who deny the Truth!
2 I do not worship what you worship,
3 And neither do you worship what I worship.
4 And I will not worship what you have worshipped.
5 And neither will you worship what I worship.
6 To you your religion, and to me my religion.

Test your knowledge of the script

1 Point out the places where the maddah occurs in this sūrah, and say why it occurs.
2 Why is there no sukūn on the nūn in أنتم (line 5)? How is this nūn pronounced:
a. indistinctly with ghunnah, or
b. distinctly without lingering?
3 What does the small oval shape on the last alif in أنا (line 6) indicate?
4 Why is the dāl in عبدتم (line 6) written bare, without a sukūn?
5 Why is the tanwīn in عابد (line 6) written in a staggered fashion?

For answers to:

question 1, see Unit 31; question 2, see Unit 42;
question 3, see Unit 37; question 4, see Unit 40;
question 5, see Unit 42.

سُورَةُ الكَافِرُونَ

بِسْمِ ٱللَّهِ ٱلرَّحْمَٰنِ ٱلرَّحِيمِ

قُلْ يَٰٓأَيُّهَا ٱلْكَٰفِرُونَ ﴿١﴾

لَآ أَعْبُدُ مَا تَعْبُدُونَ ﴿٢﴾

وَلَآ أَنتُمْ عَٰبِدُونَ مَآ أَعْبُدُ ﴿٣﴾

وَلَآ أَنَا۠ عَابِدٌ مَّا عَبَدتُّمْ ﴿٤﴾

وَلَآ أَنتُمْ عَٰبِدُونَ مَآ أَعْبُدُ ﴿٥﴾

لَكُمْ دِينُكُمْ وَلِىَ دِينِ ﴿٦﴾

S<u>u</u>rah an-Nasr

Help

In the name of Allāh, the Most Gracious, the Ever Merciful

1 When God's help comes, and victory,
2 And you see people entering the religion of God in multitudes,
3 Celebrate, then, the praise of your Sustainer, and seek His forgiveness.
4 He is ever ready to accept repentance.

Test your knowledge of the script

1. Why is there a maddah on the alif in جاء (line 3)?
2. When pausing at the end of verse 1, make sure the ḥa' is pronounced with a strong expulsion of breath.
3. When pausing at the end of verse 2, how is أفواجا pronounced?
4. When pausing at the end of verse 3, how is توابا pronounced?
5. Point out two instances of a nūn with a shaddah. How is this nūn pronounced?

For answers to:

question 1, see Unit 31; question 2, see Unit 6; question 3, see Unit 43; question 4, see Unit 43; question 5, see Unit 21.

سُورَةُ النَّصۡرِ

بِسۡمِ ٱللَّهِ ٱلرَّحۡمَٰنِ ٱلرَّحِيمِ

إِذَا جَآءَ نَصۡرُ ٱللَّهِ وَٱلۡفَتۡحُ ١

وَرَأَيۡتَ ٱلنَّاسَ

يَدۡخُلُونَ فِي دِينِ ٱللَّهِ أَفۡوَاجٗا ٢

فَسَبِّحۡ بِحَمۡدِ رَبِّكَ وَٱسۡتَغۡفِرۡهُۚ

إِنَّهُۥ كَانَ تَوَّابَۢا ٣

S<u>u</u>rah al-Masad

Twisted Strands

In the name of Allah, the Most Gracious, the Ever Merciful

1 Doomed are the hands (the power) of Abū Lahab,
and doomed is He.
2 His wealth and what he has gained will not benefit him.
3 (In the life to come), he shall burn in a fire of fierce flames,
4 Together with his wife, as the carrier of firewood (evil tales and slander),
5 Around whose neck is a rope of twisted strands.

Test your knowledge of the script

1. Why is there a maddah on the alif in يدا (line 3)?
2. Point out one instance of incomplete assimilation *(idghām nāqiṣ).*
3. What is the last letter in أغنى (line 4) called?
4. Point out two instances in one line of complete assimilation *(idghām kāmil).*
5. Point out the three instances of a mīm having a shaddah. How should this mīm be pronounced?
6. Why is there a sukūn on the nūn in عنه (line 4) and no sukūn on the nūn in من (line 7)? How is each nūn pronounced:
   a. indistinctly with ghunnah, or
   b. distinctly without lingering, or
   c. completely dropped in pronunciation?
7. With what type of letter do all the verses in this sūrah end?

For answers to:

question 1, see Unit 31; question 2, see Unit 41;
question 3, see Unit 24; question 4, see Unit 39;
question 5, see Units 21 & 39; question 6, see Units 38 & 39;
question 7, see Unit 17.

سُورَةُ المَسَدِ

بِسْمِ ٱللَّهِ ٱلرَّحْمَٰنِ ٱلرَّحِيمِ

تَبَّتْ يَدَآ أَبِي لَهَبٍ وَتَبَّ ﴿١﴾

مَآ أَغْنَىٰ عَنْهُ مَالُهُۥ وَمَا كَسَبَ ﴿٢﴾

سَيَصْلَىٰ نَارًا ذَاتَ لَهَبٍ ﴿٣﴾

وَٱمْرَأَتُهُۥ حَمَّالَةَ ٱلْحَطَبِ ﴿٤﴾

فِي جِيدِهَا حَبْلٌ مِّن مَّسَدٍۭ ﴿٥﴾

Su͟rah al-Ikhlaas

Purity of Faith

In the name of Allāh, the Most Gracious, the Ever Merciful

1 Say: He, *Allāh*, is One!
2 Allah, the Eternal, the Absolute.
3 He begets not nor was He begotten.
4 And there is none that could be compared with Him.

Test your knowledge of the script

1 Why is there no sukūn on the nūn in يكن له (line 6)?
This bare nūn is :
a. pronounced indistinctly with ghunnah, or
b. pronounced distinctly without lingering, or
c. completely dropped in pronunciation?

2 Why is the tanwīn in كفوا written as it is? This tanwin is pronounced:
a. indistinctly with ghunnah, or
b. distinctly without lingering.

3 All the verses in this sūrah end with a daal which is a ______ letter.

For answers to:

question 1, see Unit 39; question 2, see Unit 14;
question 3, see Unit 17.

سُورَةُ الإِخْلَاصِ

بِسْمِ ٱللَّهِ ٱلرَّحْمَٰنِ ٱلرَّحِيمِ

قُلْ هُوَ ٱللَّهُ أَحَدٌ ﴿١﴾

ٱللَّهُ ٱلصَّمَدُ ﴿٢﴾

لَمْ يَلِدْ وَلَمْ يُولَدْ ﴿٣﴾

وَلَمْ يَكُن لَّهُۥ كُفُوًا أَحَدٌۢ ﴿٤﴾

S<u>u</u>rah al-Falaq

The Rising Dawn

In the name of Allāh, the Most Gracious, the Ever Merciful
1 Say: I seek refuge with the Sustainer of the rising dawn,
2 From the evil of what He created,
3 From the evil of the darkness when it descends,
4 From the evil of those steeped in occult practices,
5 And from the evil of an envious one when he envies.

Test your knowledge of the script

1 Why is there no sukūn on the nūn in من شر (lines 4-7)?
This bare nūn is:
a. pronounced indistinctly with ghunnah, or
b. pronounced distinctly without lingering, or
c. completely dropped in pronunciation?

2 Why is the tanwīn in غاسق and حاسد written as it is? This tanwin is pronounced:
a. indistinctly with ghunnah, or
b. distinctly without lingering?

3 All the verses in this sūrah end with a ق, ب or د. These are all ________ letters.

For answers to:

question 1, see Unit 42; question 2, see Unit 14;
question 3, see Unit 17.

سُورَةُ الفَلَقِ

بِسْمِ ٱللَّهِ ٱلرَّحْمَٰنِ ٱلرَّحِيمِ

قُلْ أَعُوذُ بِرَبِّ ٱلْفَلَقِ ﴿١﴾

مِن شَرِّ مَا خَلَقَ ﴿٢﴾

وَمِن شَرِّ غَاسِقٍ إِذَا وَقَبَ ﴿٣﴾

وَمِن شَرِّ ٱلنَّفَّٰثَٰتِ فِى ٱلْعُقَدِ ﴿٤﴾

وَمِن شَرِّ حَاسِدٍ إِذَا حَسَدَ ﴿٥﴾

S<u>u</u>rah an-Naas

Humankind

In the name of Allāh, the Most Gracious, the Ever Merciful

1 Say: I seek refuge with the Sustainer of humankind,
2 The Sovereign of humankind,
3 The God of humankind,
4 From the evil of the sneaking whisperer,
5 Who whispers into the hearts of humans,
6 From among both jinn and humans.

Test your knowledge of the script

1. Each verse in this sūrah has a nūn with a shaddah. How is a nūn with a shaddah pronounced?
2. Why is there no sukūn on the nūn in من شر (line 6)?
   This bare nūn is:
   a. pronounced indistinctly with ghunnah, or
   b. pronounced distinctly without lingering, or
   c. completely dropped in pronunciation.

For answers to:

question 1, see Unit 21; question 2, see Unit 42.

سُورَةُ النَّاسِ

بِسْمِ ٱللَّهِ ٱلرَّحْمَٰنِ ٱلرَّحِيمِ

قُلْ أَعُوذُ بِرَبِّ ٱلنَّاسِ ﴿١﴾

مَلِكِ ٱلنَّاسِ ﴿٢﴾

إِلَٰهِ ٱلنَّاسِ ﴿٣﴾

مِن شَرِّ ٱلْوَسْوَاسِ ٱلْخَنَّاسِ ﴿٤﴾

ٱلَّذِى يُوَسْوِسُ فِى صُدُورِ ٱلنَّاسِ ﴿٥﴾

مِنَ ٱلْجِنَّةِ وَٱلنَّاسِ ﴿٦﴾

SECTION NINE

Glossary & Appendices

Glossary

Alif Maqṣūrah. An alif written as ى when it occurs at the end of a word, or as ـبـ or ـيـ when it is in the middle of a word and preceded by a letter with a fat-ḥah.

Assimilation. The complete or partial dropping of one letter in pronunciation when followed by a letter from a close point of articulation, e.g. the dropping of a 'l' followed by an 'r'. Also called 'merging'.

Complete Merging. (Arabic: *idghām kāmil*). The dropping of a final vowel-less ن when followed by a word beginning with a ر ل م or ن, e.g: مِن رَّبِّ is pronounced *mir rab bi.*
Complete merging with humming or *ghunnah* (Arabic: *idghām bi-ghunnah*). Occurs when the vowelless ن is followed by mīm or nūn.
Complete merging without humming or ghunnah (Arabic: *idghām bi-ghayri ghunnah*). Occurs when the vowelless ن is followed by rau or lām.

Consonant. Any of the speech sounds made by partly or completely stopping the flow of air as it goes through the organs of speech. With the exception of the bare ا , و and ى , when used as long vowels, all Arabic lettters are consonants.
A hamzah written on its own or with an alif is a consonant.

Conversion. (Iqlāb). The pronunciation of ن as م when followed by a ب , e.g. جَنْبِ pronounced *jambi.*

Ḍammah. The short vowel 'u' written as a hook or large comma above a letter and sounded as the *u* in *full.*

Diphthong. A vowel sound, part of a single syllable, during which the tongue moves from one position to another, causing a continual change in vowel quality, eg. the vowel 'a' moving to the sound of the vowel 'i' produces the diphthong 'ay' - as in the word بَيْت ; or the vowel 'a' moving to the sound of the vowel 'u' produces the diphthong 'aw' - as in the word مَوْت .

Fat-ḥah. The short vowel 'a' sounded either as the *a* in *cat,* the *a* in *hart* or the *o* in *cot* depending on the letter above which it occurs; written as a small slanting stroke above a letter.

Ghunnah. A pleasant humming nasal sound prolonged to two lengths or ḥarakahs.

Hamzatu- qaṭ'. The character (ء) which is written on its own or with an alif, yā' without dots, or wāw. It is always pronounced regardless of its position in speech. It is sometimes referred to as the glottal stop and pronounced from the throat as a very slight cough or a 'catch' in the breath.

Hamzatu-l Waṣl. The 'connecting

hamzah' written as أ . It is pronounced only when it comes at the beginning of an utterance; otherwise, it is not pronounced.

Ḥarakah. A 'beat' or standard time unit of estimating vowel length or the extent of prolonging a vowel. A vowel may be lengthened to two ḥarakahs which is roughly the time it takes to move the thumb from the tips of the index finger to the middle finger. Four ḥarakahs is roughly the time taken to move the thumb from the index finger to the little finger.

Idghām. See Merging

Idghām Kāmil. Complete merging

Idghām Nāqiṣ. Incomplete merging

Incomplete merging. The partial

dropping of a final vowelless ن before an initial و or يـ . The و or يـ is partially doubled and pronounced with ghunnah, the humming nasal sound.

Ikhfā' . Means 'concealing or lowering'. Refers to the indistinct pronunciation of an 'n' sound when it is followed by letters other than the iẓhār letters, the idghām letters or bā'. In other words, the ikhfā' letters are:

ت ث ج د ذ ز س ش
ص ض ط ظ ف ق ك

Kasrah. The short vowel 'i' sounded as the *i* in *pin* and written as a small slanting stroke below a letter.

Long vowel. A vowel two ḥarakahs long. The long vowels *aa*, *ii* and *uu* are indicated by a bare alif, yā' and wāw after a fat-ḥah, kasrah and ḍammah respectively.

Maddah. A wavy sign (~) over a long vowel letter indicating that the long vowel letter must, or can, be prolonged to the length of four or six ḥarakahs.

Merging. The merging of two adjacent sounds when pronounced in sequence. See 'Complete merging' and 'Incomplete merging'.

Moon Letters. See 'Qamarī Letters'.

Nasal. From the nose. The sound of the mīm and nūn produced by closure of the mouth so that air is free to pass out through the nose.

Qalqalah. Refers to the 'shakiness' produced by extra emphasis on certain letters at the end of an utterance. or when these letters have a sukūn. The 'qalqalah'

letters are: ق ط ب ج د

contained in the words قُطْب جَد.
The reason for the extra stress on these letters is that they should not be mistaken for similar sounding letters.

Glossary

Qamarī Letter. A 'moon' letter which allows the ل of the definite article ألْ to have a sukūn and be pronounced when that letter comes directly after the ل. Qaf is an example of a 'moon' letter as in ٱلْقَمَر, meaning 'the moon'.

Shaddah. A (ـّ) sign placed over a letter. A shaddah (1) joins and (2) doubles. It joins in pronunciation the letter above which it occurs to the previous letter and vowel to form one syllable. It then doubles the letter above which it occurs.

Shamsī Letter. See 'Sun Letters'. A letter which takes a shaddah when attached to the definite article ألْ , the ل of which is left bare and dropped in pronunciation.

Short Vowel. A vowel which is one ḥarakah long. The three short vowels are: fat-ḥah ـَ; kasrah ـِ; ḍammah ـُ.

Sukūn. The absence of a vowel sound on a consonant, denoted by the sign ـْ.

Sun Letters. Named after the word 'shamsī' meaning 'sun'.
A 'Sun Letter' takes a shaddah when attached to the definite article ألْ , the ل of which is left bare and not pronounced.

The 'sun letters' are (from right to left):

ت ث د ذ ر ز س ش ص ض ط ظ ل ن

Tanwīn. Adding an 'n' sound at the ending of a word. Tanwīn is usually indicated by doubling the short vowel.
Tanwīn with the vowel 'a' (ـً) is called 'fat-ḥah tanwīn'.
Tanwīn with the vowel 'i' (ـٍ) is called 'kasrah tanwīn'.
Tanwīn with the vowel 'u' (ـٌ) is called 'ḍammah tanwīn'.

Tajwīd. The art and the science of reciting the Qur'ān in a manner that each letter and syllable is pronounced accurately and precisely with proper attention to such matters as correct vowel lengths and the rules of pausing.

Transliteration. Writing the sounds or letters of one language in the alphabet of another, e.g. the Arabic letter ث is transliterated into English as '*th*'; the Arabic word قرءان is transliterated into English as *Qur'ān*.

Vowel. A voiced sound produced when breath is let out freely without any stop or closing of the air passage.

Verse numbers

Verse numbers are given in a circle at the end of each verse or *ayah*. The number of verses or āyāt in the Qur'ān is 6236.
The Arabic numerals from 1 - 10 are *(read from right to left):*

١٠ ٩ ٨ ٧ ٦ ٥ ٤ ٣ ٢ ١

In English, as in Arabic, units are written on the right of a number, then tens, hundreds etc., as in:

19 = ١٩ 105 = ١٠٥
487 = ٤٨٧ 6236 = ٦٢٣٦.

Thirty Juz'

For the convenience of the reciter, the Qur'ān was divided by later scholars into thirty Juz' or parts. Each Juz' is named after the first word with which it starts. For example, the first Juz' is called *Alif Lām Mīm* and the last Juz is called *Juz' 'Amma.*

At the beginning of a Juz', a decorative sign appears in the margin with the number of the Juz' and the number of the Ḥizb.

الجزء ٣
الحزب ٥

These words indicate the beginning of the third Juz' and the fifth Ḥizb.

Sixty Hizb

Each Juz' is sub-divided into two parts, each part called a Ḥizb. There are thus 60 ḥizb in the Qur'ān. A sign with the word al-ḥizb is put in the margin with the number of the ḥizb. Each ḥizb in turn is divided into four quarters.

Quarter (rub'u) of a Hizb

At the end of the first quarter of a ḥizb, a decorative sign is shown in the margin with the words *rub'u al ḥizb* followed by the number of the ḥizb below.

ربع
الحزب
٦٠

Half (nisf) of a Hizb

At the end of the first half of a ḥizb, the same decorative sign is shown with the words *niṣf al ḥizb* and the ḥizb number below.

نصف
الحزب
٦٠

Three quarters of a Hizb

At the end of the three quarters of a ḥizb, the decorative sign is shown with the words *thalaathatu arba'a al ḥizb* and the ḥizb number below.

ثلاثة أرباع
الحزب
٦٠

At the beginning of each Juz', Ḥizb, and of each quarter of a Ḥizb, the sign ۞ is placed within the text. This sign does not occur when the Juz' starts at the beginning of a sūrah.

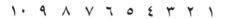

Appendix 2

How to use this book

Any person, from at least age seven onwards, should be able to acquire the basic skills of reading and writing the vowelled Arabic script in a few weeks of focussed learning. Fluency, with all the attention to detail that is required, will come with much and constant practice. Reading and writing, however, must be preceded by listening and imitating precise, accurate recitation.

A marvel

It is one of the marvels of Arabic, that non-Arabic speaking peoples can learn to read and recite the Qur'ān accurately whether they are able to understand it or not. This is no doubt due to the precision and beauty of the Arabic script and the reverence which the Qur'ān as the word of God inspires.

Learners, from a very early age, need to be exposed to the authentic sounds of Arabic through listening to good recitations either from individuals or from recordings. Recordings on cassette tapes, CDs, and CD Roms with the facility of repetition on striking a key are now widely available.

To stress the value of listening and repeating, this book is accompanied by recordings on CDs and audio tapes. For both teachers and learners, the whole process of learning to read the Qur'ān should be an enjoyable one.

This book can be used by an absolute beginner. It can be used for self-study and also for learning with a class or a group. For the best results, it is suggested that courses in reading and writing the Arabic script and reading the Qur'ān should be taught intensively over a period of three to four weeks, four or five days a week and about two hours a day.

Students and indeed teachers need to be well motivated. The importance of learning Arabic and reading and understanding the Qur'ān should be stressed.

Students need to be given confidence. They should be able to realise, through a feeling of early achievement, that the Arabic script is not something strange and difficult. It is precise and elegant and not riddled with variations and exceptions in spelling and pronunciation as in English. It should be both relatively easy and great fun to learn to read and write it.

Self-study

For self-study, users need to go through Section One of the book as quickly as possible, preferably in two or three days.

Listen to the recording of Unit 1 and follow the Arabic text. Each line of text is identified. Pause the recording and read the notes

for the Unit on the facing page.
Listen to the recording again and repeat the sounds clearly. Repeat as many times as necessary to reproduce the sounds and to understand the principles involved in combining letters and vowels to produce syllables and words.

All letters introduced in Section One have almost exact equivalents in English and should therefore be quite easy for an English speaking person. The main vowels and signs are introduced in this Section.

Section One of this Textbook is designed to be used with Workbook One of *Easy Steps in Arabic Handwriting*. Writing should be started immediately after completing Section One of the Textbook and listening to Units 1 to 5 on the recording.

For classroom use and intensive courses

Teachers need to emphasize the importance of Arabic for Muslims: with regard to the Qur'ān, the performance of Ṣalāt and Muslim unity.

Variety of techniques

Teachers need to use a variety of materials, techniques and skills in teaching the Arabic script.

1 Teacher reads, students listen. (May be done three or four times.)
2 Teacher reads, students repeat (three times).
3 Teacher points out characteristics of each letter: shape, whether with or without dot(s); relation to the base line when writing etc.
4 Teacher and students read.
5 Individual students are asked to read.
6 Teacher shows how each letter is written. Students practice writing.

The recording may be used in any of stages 1-2 in place of the teacher.

It is not necessary that students should completely master a rule or a page before going on to a succeeding lesson. Staying with one rule or lesson too long leads to boredom and lack of achievement. A quick pressing on with the rules and reading practice may be somewhat confusing initially but soon contributes to a sense of achievement. From the first day of a course, students should be able to read and write Arabic words.

Constant revision and testing

Constant revision and testing must be a feature of any course. The methods need to be varied to create and maintain interest and enjoyment. Repetition by the teacher, oral and individual questioning to test accurate pronunciation and knowledge of rules, the use of the tape recorder and frequent dictation practice as a group or by individual students writing on the classroom board - these are examples of varying techniques.

Appendix 2: How to use this book

Concentration and discipline

Any effective teaching and learning cannot proceed unless the teacher maintains total control of the class while at the same time maintaining a completely relaxed, and pleasant atmosphere. Switching from one activity to another helps to maintain concentration and discipline.

Listening and choral repetition, individuals reading in sequence, dictation practice, use of overhead projector or computer for rapid revision, requesting students to perform the role of teacher, games with flashcards, short breaks for exercise, snacks and intervals for Ṣalāh - all contribute to maintaining the relaxed but disciplined atmosphere necessary for learning.

Homework

Homework, both reading and writing, needs to be given for every day of the course. Homework can be: revision of work done in the class, through use of recordings or computer at home; completion of writing in the Workbook, copying verses and sūrahs, or writing of short sūrahs from memory.

Suggestions for further reading and study

Emphasize regular daily reading of the Qur'ān.

Listen to good recitations of the Qur'ān like those of Al-Minshāwī, Al-Husarī, Muḥammad Jibrīl, and others.

The use of the book *Tajwīd al-Qur'ān* by Ashraf Abdul-Fattah and others is highly recommended as a detailed reference.

Students then need to work towards understanding Qur'ānic Arabic through a programme of regular and systematic study. The MELS *Access to Qur'ānic Arabic* course may be useful in this respect and contains suggestions for further study.

Regular group study

Arrange for regular group study and reading of the Qur'ān, at a local mosque, community centre, weekend camp, school or home.

This is just the beginning - the beginning of a rewarding and enjoyable journey of discovering and living by the Qur'ān.

Notes

Notes